Giftedness:
Discovering
Your Areas of Strength

Giftedness:

Discovering Your Areas of Strength

Marcia L. Mitchell

BETHANY HOUSE PUBLISHERS
MINNEAPOLIS, MINNESOTA 55438
A Division of Bethany Fellowship, Inc.

Published by Bethany House Publishers
A Division of Bethany Fellowship, Inc.
6820 Auto Club Road, Minneapolis, Minnesota 55438

Printed in the United States of America

Library of Congress Cataloging-in-Publication Data

Mitchell, Marcia, 1942–
    Giftedness : discovering your areas of strength.

    1. Women—Religious life. 2. Gifts, Spiritual.
3. Women in church work. I. Title.
BV4527.M544 1988   248.8'43   88-1211
ISBN 0-87123-995-7 (pbk.)

For my husband, Fred,
who lovingly supports
whatever I'm doing

MARCIA L. MITCHELL is a free-lance writer who is active as a seminar leader at writers' conferences and has taught writing on a college level. Besides her published books *Spiritually Single* and *Jenny*, and a long list of published articles, she has also served as an advisory board member for the Northwest Region of Wycliffe Bible Translators and is presently studying toward ordination in the ministry. Her family includes two grown girls, and she and her husband live in Walla Walla, Washington.

TABLE OF CONTENTS

Chapter 1 Living Sacrifices 13
Chapter 2 With Strings Attached 27
Chapter 3 The Leading Edge..................... 43
Chapter 4 An Apple for the Teacher............. 59
Chapter 5 Encourage One Another 73
Chapter 6 Blessed Are the Merciful.............. 89
Chapter 7 Giving With Joy 103
Chapter 8 Serving With Love....................119
Chapter 9 Your Sons and Daughters Will
            Prophesy 133
Chapter 10 Uniquely You 147
Chapter 11 Where Do I Fit?......................159
Appendix A 173
Appendix B 181

INTRODUCTION

Serving Jesus with joy! That's what this book is about. We'll discuss how to find what you like to do, what you do best, and where you fit in God's plan.

Nothing is as frustrating as trying to serve God while feeling discouraged or inadequate. But each of us has things she can do and do well that will please God and bring enjoyment in the process.

Do you feel frustrated at what you are doing? Do you wish you could be involved in some other activity? You are not alone. Many daughters of God are serving Him in quiet desperation. Stymied and stale, they plod along, just getting the job done. Each of us needs to find a comfortable niche for serving Jesus.

Relax. You can *know* where you belong. You can find out exactly where you fit. Let's work through it together. Many of the women mentioned in this book started their personal search for satisfying service while they were frustrated, just like you.

LIVING SACRIFICES

CHAPTER ONE

"I guess I'll have to work in the nursery after all," said author/pastor's wife Janet Bly. Her husband Steve had accepted their first pastorate, and she was having difficulty finding her niche. She knew the nursery provided a very important service to parents in the congregation, but it just didn't "fit" her. Instead of joy, it brought frustration. Then, after exploring various areas of ministry for two years, God opened the door for her unique writing career.

One day while typing up Steve's sermons, she recognized an intriguing story buried in his text. She unearthed it, polished it, and sent it to a publisher. That was the beginning of a productive writing ministry for the two of them. Together they have written many articles and books that have touched hearts far beyond the members of their local congregation.

Janet could have continued to struggle in the whirlpool of doing whatever happened to come along. But she chose, at her husband's urging, to seek her own place of service, a special task that God wanted her to do.

Many women, as Janet did, are just "doing a job" because they've been asked or because "somebody has to do it." Often they are unhappy or unfulfilled. But it doesn't have to be that way.

For years I was part of a team that taught the third-grade Sunday school class. I did it because:

a. Someone asked me to do it.

b. The need was there and I thought I should do it.

c. I didn't know what else to do.

But I didn't enjoy it. The storytelling was O.K., but I never developed a rapport with the kids like some of the other teachers had. I did the job I was given in the manner I was instructed, but it wasn't much fun. (I'll bet the kids didn't think it was fun, either.)

No one told me work in the church could be enjoyable. But I've discovered that if we are doing what God intends for us to do, it should bring joy to us as well as to the others involved.

Finding a channel of service you can love sometimes seems impossible. But think about it for a minute. Do you think Jesus was bored by his ministry? Do you think Paul got up each morning and groaned, "Oh no, not another day with those Gentiles!"? Of course not. (Well, maybe once in a while, although Scripture doesn't record it, but that just makes him more human, right?)

The excitement Jesus felt at doing His Father's will is evident in both His words and His actions. Paul knew exactly what God was asking him to do, and he did it with obvious enthusiasm.

That's the way all our service should be—filled with excitement and enthusiasm. Even on the ordinary days when things seem to just plod along, there should still be a sense of joy. If you love your area of service, the joy will be there.

Why should anyone bother to find something special to do? Isn't it enough to accept Christ as our Savior? We attend church more often than most people. We follow the moral standards of Christ's teachings. We may even tithe and sing in the choir.

Why should anyone bother to find a new or different task? Maybe you can say, "I've taught a Sunday school class for forty years; why should I change now?"

As you read through this book, you may find you don't have to change, especially if you enjoy what you are doing. You may learn that you are already effectively using the gifts God has given you for ministry. However, you may also discover a new challenge, a new and perhaps unique area of service that may stir your blood.

Possibly you are frustrated in what you are currently doing because you know you aren't using your strongest gift. Does that mean you can't do anything unless it is your number-one gift from God? Of course not. There are times when we all must do whatever task is at hand. We have to wait for God's timing to move into other areas.

Perhaps you are caught by family responsibilities or circumstances that simply don't allow you to do what you know you do best. Try to remember that raising a family doesn't last forever. If you have small children, or big ones, your focus now is on training them. Later, when your children have left home, you'll move on to other things.

If you are hedged in by current circumstances that don't allow you to perform the service you know you'd like to do, then use this waiting time wisely. Perhaps this is the time for you to add some training that would prepare you for a future ministry or area of service. If you are "on hold," then remember: God has everything under control. Wait for Him to lead you.

It's easy to become bogged down with guilt when we

see a need and can't help. Sometimes it seems the needs are so great, but we don't have enough hands, or feet, or hours in the day to do it all.

God doesn't expect you to do it all! He expects you to do only what He asks. He won't give you more to do than you can handle.

God used the gifts of a dear Christian friend to help me discover a new challenge.

Fern is my best friend. She is as tall (or I should say, as short) as I am, pencil thin, and walks vigorously about four miles every day. She says I eat too many sweets, weigh ten pounds more than I should, and need more exercise. She prays with me, takes me for walks when I'd rather not, and keeps me from buying candy bars when I'm absolutely famished! Still she is my best friend!

When I'm hurting, she listens; when I'm starting down the wrong path or making a bad choice, she points it out to me in plain English. In other words . . . she is my *best* friend!

Fern is also an artist. With a few short strokes of her brush and a dab of color, she can turn a piece of canvas into my favorite view of the Blue Mountains.

One day, on one of our never-ending walks, I complained about how unfair it seemed that God gave her all that talent and He passed me by. Instead of comforting me, my friend Fern said, "Don't try to copy me. Do whatever God gave you to do. Your hands paint pictures with words and mine use paint, but the results are both equal in God's sight."

Not long after that on another long walk, I complained that there were no books written for women whose husbands aren't Christians. There were books on how to have a beautiful Christian marriage, how to raise a fantastic Christian family, but nothing that fit my specific needs.

You know what Fern's response was? She said, "Instead of complaining about it . . . write one yourself.''

Now, I'd been writing little things for magazines and children's Sunday school papers, but write a book? The idea was preposterous.

Yet the thought just wouldn't go away. If I was hurting, surely there were other women out there who were hurting, too. The more I thought about it, the more I realized that I'd learned some valuable lessons over the years, and I'd made some glorious mistakes that I would love to help other people avoid.

And Fern wouldn't let the idea die.

One day on our walk we went into a store and Fern introduced me to a young woman. Almost the first thing that woman said to me was, ''I'm going to divorce my husband and marry a Christian. I'm tired of living like this.''

The shock was overwhelming! I wanted to shout, ''No, you don't have to do it! There are ways you can live a victorious Christian life even if your husband doesn't share your beliefs.'' But she dashed out the door, and it was too late for me to help her.

As we walked out of that store, Fern's first words to me were, ''Now do you see why you have to write that book? People out there desperately need it. It isn't that you have anything special to say, or any unique revelations from God, but you need to be willing to risk sharing with others what God is doing for you. Maybe it will give them the courage to keep trying.''

You see, Fern is not only a Spirit-filled artist, she also has the gift of encouragement.

From that day on, she would always ask me how many pages I'd written. She would challenge me and push me until finally the book was done.

God gave me gifts and talents to use in His name, but He also gave me a friend with gifts that complement mine and help me fulfill His plan. That's how we fit together.

God has given each of us gifts that He intends us to use to glorify His name. Whatever your gifts are, whatever God has given you to do, do it.

Rom. 11:29 is true: "God's gifts and his call are irrevocable" (NIV). If He has called you to a certain task, you can't deny it. It wells up inside you and you simply have to do it.

I didn't write my books alone. There were people like Fern who influenced me, people whom God used to help me get started, people who kept me going and encouraged me.

But there is one lady in my life who has no idea that she shares in the ministry of my books.

Mrs. Keck was an old lady in 1945. At least to me she was old, although I don't really know her age. I must have been about two or three years old when I started wandering the half block from my house to her flower garden. A white picket fence marched along the sidewalk where I squatted to smell her flowers.

I still treasure a photograph I have of the two of us standing in a bed of iris blooms. Mrs. Keck was tall and thin, and her white hair, piled in a coil on top of her head, set off her wrinkled face. She lived in a neat but shabby white board house.

By the time I was five we had developed a wonderful friendship. She often invited me to her house to pop popcorn over the old wood stove in the back kitchen. Nothing fancy for us, she used a wire basket on a long wooden handle.

Several times I can remember standing on a box at the back of her chair while she let down her braids. Then, ever so carefully, I'd brush that long, long hair. It was a special moment for both of us. She had no grandchildren, and my only living grandmother was too far away for me to visit.

I don't know exactly when she first started taking my brother and me to Sunday school, but it was probably sometime during the fifth year of my life. By the following May, just a few days before my sixth birthday, I clearly remember kneeling at the front pew of our tiny church and giving my heart to Jesus. Not only was I saved that day, a few minutes later my mother also knelt beside me and began her own new life in Christ.

It may have seemed a small thing for Mrs. Keck to make friends with a lonely little girl and invite her to Sunday school. This was an act of mercy done quietly and without fanfare. But if Mrs. Keck hadn't listened to God, hadn't allowed Him to minister to me through her gift of mercy, I wouldn't have grown up knowing Christ. And I wouldn't have written Christian books.

In The Living Bible, Zech. 4:10 says, "Do not despise this small beginning, for the eyes of the Lord rejoice to see the work begin." No matter what gifts God has given you, you are to start where you are—even if it's something as small as taking a neighbor child to Sunday school.

Mrs. Keck often encouraged me (another of her gifts) to keep on going to Sunday school and to learn Scripture. She did these acts because they were her way of expressing God. She had no idea that nearly forty years later, the little girl who loved to smell the flowers would extend that expression of God's love to others across the nation and world who were hurting.

Our gifts multiply when we use them. As they blend with the gifts God gives to others, they grow. Think of each gift as a puzzle piece. By itself, each piece has a unique shape and color. It doesn't take up much space on the table, nor does it show much of the picture. But put it together with other pieces and suddenly it takes on a sparkling new meaning. The tiniest piece fuses with other pieces and melts into the whole. Then, the picture vibrates with meaning.

Gayle is another woman who has found a quiet and enjoyable area in which to express God's love.

Gayle is a lady with a large smile and a happy heart who loves to help people. You never know how many teenagers will be draped across her living room furniture or what current project paraphernalia will be piled in her sewing/crafts corner. She is constantly making something, whether it's a dress for a handicapped child or a floral arrangement for the sanctuary.

But most of all, Gayle loves weddings.

She can smell a wedding brewing so far in advance that by the time the happy couple announce their engagement, she has already started a file with lots of ideas for their ceremony. But even if she's caught unaware, Gayle can still pull a wedding together and make it run so smoothly that people think it's been planned for months.

When our daughter suddenly decided on a Mother's Day wedding only ten days away, Gayle's first words to me were, "Just relax." She brewed a cup of tea for me, and while I sipped it, she stirred through her craft box. By the time I'd finished nibbling on a cookie, she handed me a lovely wedding bouquet for the bride.

In those ten short days she created a lovely wedding for all of us. No detail was ignored, no last-minute problem too difficult; she proved her dual gifts of Serving and Administration. One of the special things she said to me was, "This wedding will always bring glory to God's name because whenever your daughter thinks of her wedding, she'll remember the church family that made it so special."

Gayle loves God and shows it through serving others. The beautiful thirteenth chapter of 1 Corinthians points to the best characteristic we can cultivate in our lives. "The greatest of these is love." It doesn't matter what your gifts are, God's love expressed through you is the greatest ministry of all. We are to love one another; we are to honor others above ourselves.

Remember that God gives His gifts according to His discernment. He knows where you live, where you are spiritually, and what the needs of the body of Christ are. He knows what you can and can't do. He won't ask you to do something that is impossible.

Karen is a woman who believes that with God nothing and no one is impossible. She can't stop telling others about Jesus. Wherever she goes, she finds opportunities to talk with strangers and lead them to Christ. It's no problem for her to knock on a door to find out if the people go to church or know about Jesus.

For many of us, that would be scary, but it's just natural for Karen—natural because she is using her God-given gift of prophecy.

Her enthusiasm for Jesus bubbles over in every conversation. Someone can mention the weather (cold or hot, snow or sun) and she turns it into an opportunity to share about Jesus. And she wants others to know how to do it, too. So, she started teaching (another of her gifts) a class in witnessing and evangelism in her church. In this way her gift is multiplied as others learn how to evangelize and join her in leading people to Christ.

Last month she read an article in our newspaper which stated that a well-known cult would be holding a convention in a small community near here. Karen organized her class and began a systematic campaign to contact as many homes in that community as possible.

Together they spent two full weekends prior to that convention making sure that as many people as possible knew the truth about Jesus. Karen didn't want anyone to be taken in by the cult's false doctrine because they didn't know what the Bible said. During those efforts, several people were won to the Lord who might never have been contacted otherwise.

You might say, "That's great for Karen, but don't ask me to knock on doors. It's impossible. I couldn't do that!"

Then perhaps prophecy isn't your gift, but everyone can learn some easy steps for sharing the good news about Jesus. In Scripture we are told, "Always be prepared to give an answer to everyone who asks you to give the reason for the hope that you have" (1 Pet. 3:15).

"What exactly are the gifts God gives?" you might ask. "And if God has created me to fill a position in the body of Christ, what is it? How do I know what I'm supposed to do?"

Rom. 12:6–8 says, "If a man's gift is prophesying, let him use it in proportion to his faith. If it is serving, let him serve; if it is teaching, let him teach; if it is encouraging, let him encourage; if it is contributing to the needs of others, let him give generously; if it is leadership, let him govern diligently; if it is showing mercy, let him do it cheerfully."

The gifts listed in this passage are:

1. Prophesying
2. Serving
3. Teaching
4. Encouraging
5. Giving
6. Leadership
7. Mercy

We are going to use these seven as the basis for our study. Other scriptures list many more, some of which are probably subdivisions of these seven. Scholars do not agree on how many gifts there are or how they should be listed. But for our purpose of finding an area of service, these seven basic gifts of God's grace will meet our needs.

We will look at each one in depth, search out its biblical meaning, and try to move it into our contemporary setting. Then we'll look at examples of people who are using these gifts in some wonderful areas of ministry.

As you learn about these gifts, you'll be able to discern which of their attributes are at work in you. God will confirm to you what His gifts are, but you need to explore them with an open, teachable mind. Not only will you learn about yourself, but you'll also learn about others around you. Knowing these principles will enable you to help other people find areas of service that fit the spiritual gifts God has given them. In this way you'll also be helping the body of Christ to function better.

Just as God takes individual wild flowers and blends them into a field of pastel beauty for us to enjoy, so He blends each person's gifts into a special bouquet that we might bring glory to Him.

What are your gifts? What does your special bouquet look like? I don't know. Maybe you have a large selection of Mercy flowers and only a dash of Teaching for color. Or, you may have a formal arrangement of Administration with only a few blossoms of Serving. Whatever your basket of flowers looks like, you can rest assured it is God's best for you.

You may be tempted to stop serving while you are reading this book. Perhaps you think you might be in the wrong area, or you just aren't sure what your ministry should be. By all means, keep on doing whatever you are currently doing. Allow God to use it to speak to you as you learn more about His spiritual gifts.

Remember, Rom. 11:29 says, "God's gifts and his call are irrevocable." Whatever He has given to you can't be denied or ignored. As you are serving Him, He will make known His plan for you. Whatever He is asking you to do, whether it's awesome in size or microscopic, I challenge you to do it.

No matter what gifts God has given you, you are to begin where you are with what you are. Remember that no one is 100% of any one of the gifts listed above. As you read through each of these chapters, keep in mind that you may have many or most of the qualities and traits of a gift, but you also will lack some of them. The first three traits may describe you exactly but trait number four won't portray you at all. That's just as it should be. We are a blend of many gifts. Just as God created no two snow-flakes exactly alike, He also created no two humans exactly alike.

I hope you'll take time to get alone with God and talk to Him about your place in the body of Christ. Then, when God says go, start where you are, no matter how insignificant it may appear to be. Don't despise that small beginning. Whatever God has given you to do, do it that His name may be glorified.

In chapter ten you will find your Personal Discovery Evaluation. What you learn from that section will help you move into a more effective position in the body of Christ.

Some people might call that chapter a spiritual gifts test, but I choose to call it your Personal Discovery Evaluation. In many tests there are right and wrong answers, and it is possible to fail. But there are no right or wrong answers here, and you absolutely cannot fail.

The Personal Discovery Evaluation section is only a guideline for your own personal use. By the time we've studied these seven gifts, you'll be able to evaluate yourself through statements that pertain to each area. No one but you needs to see your answers.

Please don't work on chapter ten until you've read all the chapters before it. You need the time and preparation to help you make a good evaluation.

In the final chapter we will apply the various gifts of grace to specific areas of service. There you will be able to see how your newly discovered or newly confirmed gifts can be used in the local body of Christ.

Just for the fun of it, take time to jot down which of these seven areas of ministry you think might be your major gift from God. You may be very surprised by the actual results of the Personal Discovery when you compare this answer with the final one.

I think my major gift is in the area of _____ .

In the light of God's love expressed through you, please prayerfully work through these next steps.

1. List some things you like to do (i.e.: invite people to your home for dinner, visit nursing homes, research Bible truths, work with your hands, etc.).
2. List some things people keep asking you to do because they know you do these things well. (Be honest.)
3. Name some specific things God has been talking to you about doing.
4. Although you try your best, are there things you are doing that frustrate you because they don't seem to be working out well? Name them.

Save these answers for comparison in the final chapter.

WITH STRINGS ATTACHED

CHAPTER TWO

A funny thing happened on the way to this study of spiritual gifts and their applications. I learned that in some Bible passages, the word *gifts* isn't even in the original text. That was a shock!

How can you have spiritual gifts if they don't exist?

In 1 Cor. 12:1; 14:1, 12, the actual word used is *spirituals*. To make the meaning understandable, the translators have added the word *gifts*.

However, in Rom. 12:6–8 there is a word for gifts, the word *charisma*. "We have different gifts (charisma), according to the grace given us" (v. 6). If we are to learn what our gifts are and how to use them, we'd better understand the word *gift* itself.

What Are Spiritual Gifts?

When we look up any word in the dictionary, there are usually several definitions. From these we can choose the appropriate meaning for the sentence in which the word is used. Scanning through the listed meanings of the Greek word *charisma*, we can skip "deliverance from danger" and a couple of others that aren't relevant. But we can stop at "(free) gift."

We have different *(free) gifts* according to the grace given us. In other words, this thing that we have is first of all given to us by God, freely. We didn't earn it in any way.

It's also interesting that the word *grace* in this verse is related to the word *gift*. It comes from the same root, *charis*. That means that these are grace gifts, given in kindness as a favor.

What Is the Purpose of Spiritual Gifts?

Spiritual gifts are given for a purpose. As I scanned the Greek dictionary, I found one more inspiring definition. *Charis*, the first part of that word, means "graciousness of manner or act." These gifts are a gracious act of God's divine influence on our hearts and the reflection of that influence in our lives.

Gifts are freely given as a gracious act of God to influence us so that His grace is reflected to others through us. That's quite a challenge. Sure, the gift is free. That's the only way God gives it. But in a way, there are strings attached. The gifts aren't meant to be spent on ourselves in any selfish manner. They are to be used to show the world who God is and what He is like. His personal gifts will reflect His personality: joy, liberality, love, faithfulness, etc.

Whatever gifts God gives to us, they are to be used in this same way. Graciously, we serve Him with our gifts in order to allow others to see who He really is. Other people need to see God's personality in us.

How Do We Use Our Spiritual Gifts?

If God gave us these gifts for the purpose of serving Him, how do they fit into our lives? How do they mesh with His overall plan?

"Now you are the body of Christ, and each one of you is a part of it" (1 Cor. 12:27). We've heard much about the church being the body of Christ. There have been so many books written about body life that it seems there could be nothing new to add. But we can't really talk about spiritual gifts without the perspective of how they fit together.

God's Word says that each of us is a part of the body of Christ and that the body is to be built up. "It was he who gave some to be apostles, some to be prophets, some to be evangelists, and some to be pastors and teachers, to prepare God's people for works of service, so that the body of Christ may be built up until we all reach unity in the faith and in the knowledge of the Son of God and become mature, attaining to the whole measure of the fullness of Christ" (Eph. 4:11–13).

As the body is built up, we (as part of that body) become more unified in our faith and knowledge of Jesus, and we become more mature, attaining the fullness of Christ in our lives.

"The body is a unit, though it is made up of many parts; and though all its parts are many, they form one body" (1 Cor. 12:12). The body of Christ isn't just your local church. Stretch your imagination. Think of every Christian, everywhere in the world, from the beginning of time to the ending of time. That's the body of Christ!

But how does that body work together to build itself up as a unit?

Interdependence

Rom. 12:4–6 says, "Just as each of us has one body with many members, and these members do not all have the same function, so in Christ we who are many form one body, and each member belongs to all the others. We have different gifts, according to the grace given us."

First of all, as a believer, you are part of Christ, one cell in His divine body. As His chosen cell, you fit together with other cells (people) to form your local church. Beyond that, you also blend together with wider ministries, to serve the larger body in your community, nation, and world. Finally, you, and millions of other believers in our time, join in the eternal forward surge of the entire body of Christ.

Some of your service may be within your local church and some may be completely outside its walls. That doesn't change your function. You are still serving Christ's body, no matter what He chooses for you to do.

It's obvious from these scriptures that God expects the body of Christ to *function*. All those parts aren't just to look at. Each is given for a purpose. The parts of the body are supposed to *do* something.

Rom. 12:1 says, "Therefore, I urge you, brothers, in view of God's mercy, to offer your bodies as living sacrifices, holy and pleasing to God—which is your spiritual worship."

Our worship of God consists of more than sitting on a pew. We are to be a living sacrifice. That means we have to get off the pew and do something.

I've seen some machines that move but don't accomplish anything. Remember Rube Goldberg and his wacky inventions? He created machines on which wheels turned, lights flashed, things made noise, but nothing happened. I've seen some Christians like that—lots of noise and motion, but nothing happens.

Scripture says that "to each one the manifestation of the Spirit is given for the common good" (1 Cor. 12:7). All our motion and noise is supposed to be productive and constructive, bringing about some benefit for the whole body.

I, for example, have learned from experience that it's better for the body of Christ if I am not the church pianist. When I was a child, I dutifully took music lessons. Don't misunderstand. I love music. I love to play the piano and sing in the choir, but playing piano for church services is not where my spiritual gifts are best expressed. I've learned the mechanics of reading notes and producing the proper sounds, but the music doesn't flow. I may feel the surge of music deep within me, but I've learned that what I'm feeling doesn't reach the souls of those who hear it.

One time a soloist was scheduled to sing for a program and the pianist didn't show up. The soloist asked if anyone in the audience could play the piano, but no one made a move.

Finally I got up and slid onto the piano bench. My hands were trembling as I started to hit a few notes. The soloist began, and I kept striking the keys, visibly shaking through the whole thing.

When the last feeble notes faded, the soloist said, "And now I'm supposed to sing another song. Is there someone in the audience who can play the piano?"

Embarrassing as that was, I've learned to evaluate the gifts God has given me by how they affect other people. As I have listened to the comments of others, I haven't heard of people being blessed because of my piano playing. I can *do* it, but it isn't a display case for my gifts.

We need to use our ears when we are searching for our gifts, to listen to the response of the people we are working with. We can't pay attention to only the nice words that tickle our ears. We have to listen for their heart response.

So, if the body functions best when each part does its own job, it would help to identify the parts of the body and define the job each does. That's one of the purposes of this book.

Discovering Our Gifts

We, in the flesh, cannot choose which part of the body we want to be. God does the choosing. "All these are the work of one and the same Spirit, and he gives them to each man [or woman], just as he determines" (1 Cor. 12:11).

Do you know how special you are? Do you know that God planned everything about you? He was there when you were being formed in your mother's womb, supervising, selecting, planning every nuance of your life.

In Ps. 139:13 David prayed, "You created my inmost being; you knit me together in my mother's womb." (Read verses 14–16 as well.) The word *knit* in verse 13 is actually the word used to describe the unique embroidery on the holy cloths used in the temple.

Can't you see the women preparing those special cloths for the temple? They probably sat in a circle and spread the cloth carefully in front of them. Laying out hanks of each color, they selected the exact shades suitable for the intricate designs. Think of the hours of planning and maybe days or months of perfectionistic labor that went into creating each unique pattern.

That's how God planned your life. You were woven together by God, uniquely embroidered for use in His Holy service.

As we look into His Word together throughout this study, we hope to discover some of the special coloring God has embroidered into your life. We'll learn the joys and cautions of these gifts. With a better understanding of both the positive and negative sides of the gifts, we'll gain new insight into the people who have them.

Gift vs. Ministry

There is a difference between the gift itself and how it is used. Gifts are what God gives to us; how each one is used is a service or ministry. Although related, the two are not identical. It is His responsibility to select and distribute the gifts according to His plan (1 Cor. 12:11). Our responsibility is to allow those gifts to be used through us in order to build up His body (Eph. 4:11–13).

The Right Focus

The most important consideration in our study of spiritual gifts is our relationship with Jesus. Our ministry or service is a result of our relationship, not the other way around. The Holy Spirit gives us these gifts because we are His. Our relationship with Jesus must come first before any concern over spiritual gifts.

When our focus is on our relationship with Jesus, then the natural result will be a gracious display of God's gifts through service. When we put service or ministry first, then our focus is on the *doing*, not the *being*. We are to *be* His, then allow Him to work through us. It is an awful mistake to let ministry or service come between you and your relationship with God.

As we allow our relationship with Jesus to grow, the gifts He has given us will become more and more evident.

Gift or Granted Request?

Some people talk about "asking" for a spiritual gift. My mother taught me that gifts were never to be asked for; rather, they were given at the instigation of the giver. I continued that teaching with my children. "Never ask for a gift," I've told them. "Wait until it is given to you." If that is proper earthly etiquette, then why should we confront God and *ask* for spiritual gifts?

Remember, the Scriptures say that He wove us together when we were in our mother's womb, so the gift or gifts are already there. God "gives them . . . just as he determines" (1 Cor. 12:11). I see a lot of *giving* by God but no examples of *asking*!

Paul tells us in 1 Cor. 12:31 to "eagerly desire the greater gifts." We are to *desire* spiritual gifts, but the idea of *asking* isn't included. In fact, the word *desire* suggests an eager passion.

Desire means to have warmth of feeling about something. It actually means fervent heat as in boiling liquid or the hot glow of solids. It includes the thought of being zealous. So Paul is saying, "With boiling passion, desire the greater gifts." (See also 1 Cor. 14:1.)

Rather than asking God for a specific gift that you might think is terrific, have a boiling passion for the greater gifts that God has for you. Leave the choice to Him but passionately seek to be His instrument in whatever selection of gifts He makes.

Gifts, Talents, Skills

A word of explanation might help here. We each have spiritual gifts, natural talents, and learned skills. They are not to be confused.

Just because you have a natural talent for public speaking doesn't mean you automatically have the gift of being a preacher. You may by profession be a schoolteacher, but that doesn't necessarily mean you have God's gift of teaching. *A spiritual gift is one that God gives for the purpose of building up the body of Christ (Eph. 4:12).*

Just because we have developed certain skills or deeply desire to be part of a specific ministry doesn't mean that we have God's gift in that area.

I was visiting in a church service when a middle-aged couple approached the platform to sing. I noticed the care the couple had exercised in how they were dressed. Her skirt matched his slacks, and her blouse was the same color as his shirt. Both picked up their microphones and smiled broadly at the congregation as the music began.

I relaxed, only to be snapped to attention as the lady began to sing. Quite frankly, although her husband was right on key, she was at least a half note sharp, and often more. The notes grated my ear as her voice swelled to a note-and-a-half high climax.

It was obvious the lady knew the song and had diligently practiced. The selection of music was appropriate to the service and her spirit and manner were carefully groomed. But rather than edifying the Body, she jarred our nerves. The message of the song was lost as we struggled to listen, aware only of the jagged notes.

I learned later that this dedicated lady has several other gifts that she uses lavishly for the Lord. But because her husband sings, she too wants to sing.

We need to allow God to use our whole person, our spiritual gifts *and* our natural talents as well as our learned skills.

Lila is a gentle middle-aged lady who has a ready smile for everyone. She loves to guide people along their journey with lots of encouragement (one of her gifts). Another of her obvious gifts is teaching. Whatever she does has a knack for imparting that knowledge to other people.

She had spent years teaching a children's Sunday school class when she was asked to take on the responsibility for an adult class. Never having taught at that level, Lila immediately began to hone her skills. She bought commentaries and reference works which she researched to add depth to her lessons. She enrolled in a college speech class to improve her verbal techniques. As a result, Lila's class is popular with her church.

Lila has successfully combined her spiritual gifts (teaching/encouraging) with her natural talents (pleasant personality, ability to relate well to people) and her learned skills (good communication, Bible knowledge).

God gives us gifts to use according to the needs of the body of Christ. Our gifts may vary in intensity according to the current specific needs of the local body. And as a gift is used, it becomes more developed and refined under the guidance of the Holy Spirit.

Cautions

We are always to use our gifts to serve others. They are never to be used to promote self. Any gift used selfishly becomes no more than "tinkling brass," losing its value.

We are reminded in 1 Cor. 13:1–3 that if we don't use God's gifts in love (that is, His love in us), then the gifts have absolutely no value.

A pastor once shared with me an experience with counterfeit gifts. "There are many abuses of spiritual gifts," he said, "but one of the more visible ones is the gift of prophecy.

"One day I was about to close a particularly moving service. The congregation seemed to be responding to the gentle moving of the Holy Spirit as they considered the truths of the message. Suddenly, out of the stillness, a man stood up and began proclaiming doom and destruction, shaking his fist at the group.

"Of course, the atmosphere became immediately hostile and the gentle mood was destroyed. The man claimed a direct message from God, but it was so contrary to what God had been telling me," the pastor explained, "I had to wonder just who his God was! We weren't listening to the same God."

I know how this pastor felt. I, too, have seen services disrupted by men and women who were more impressed with their own importance or more concerned about their own need for personal attention than they were in the gentle wooing of the Holy Spirit. And yet, I've also been in services where these special messages from God were spoken in His love, blending beautifully with the message God had given to the pastor.

Different but Equal

No gift is greater or lesser than another. All our gifts are equal in God's sight. They unify us in the body of Christ. They are equal in significance but uniquely different according to their function. Each one serves a different purpose, but together they enable the body of Christ to work effectively.

It's up to us to allow Him to reveal His gifts in us. Rather than "seeking" a gift, we are to grow and cultivate our relationship with Him. As we explore new ways to allow Him to work through us, He will reveal more and more of the gifts He has given.

We need to develop a certain mind-set that will allow God to use us no matter what the situation. If we can learn to say, "Lord, here am I—use me in this circumstance," then He can expand the gifts within us. When we say, "I only have the administration gift, therefore I can't be merciful," then we are hindering the work of the Holy Spirit within us. The gifts are woven into our lives, but we have to allow God to use those gifts whenever they are needed.

God has work that needs to be done, and we are His instruments. His grace, His gracious gifts, are always sufficient for the tasks He presents to us. Although you may not have an overwhelming abundance of a certain gift, God will provide exactly what is needed to accomplish His tasks. In fact, He already has.

The body of Christ is like a tapestry in progress. The threads are all there, and when God wants to utilize a certain color, though it may be at a most unexpected time, He reaches through and pulls the thread of that color to the front. We, the thread, need to be pliable and willing.

God has given us the capacity to do some things very well, but experience teaches us that we do not excel in everything. We acknowledge that we have certain limitations or "nonstrengths." That is why it is imperative for us to work interdependently with other Christians. Your strong points correspond to my weak areas. My gifts balance well with your nonstrengths.

Because of this I need to give you encouragement and space to use your strengths. In return, you need to recognize my nonstrengths and not expect magnificent performance from me in those weak areas. Our gifts blend together to build up the body of Christ.

Relational Abilities and Gifts

Each person also has differing relational abilities or capacities. How we relate to one another affects our ministry within the body of Christ. According to the IDAK Group, an organization which has specialized in evaluating individuals' God-given aptitudes, most people fit into one of three types of relational abilities.

Multi-relational

The *Multi-relational* person relates quickly and easily to people on the first encounter. She enjoys going from person to person, and usually the day is not long enough for her to relate with new ones. In most cases, repeated contact with the same people will not deepen the relationship.

Familiar Group Relational

In the second grouping is the woman who is *Familiar Group Relational.* She likes to go back to the same group of people in order to get to know them better (e.g., Sunday school class, Bible study group, ladies' fellowship, prayer group). Most people fit into this category. The more she can go back to this group, the better she gets to know them, and the more comfortable she feels.

Singular Relational

The lady who is *Singular Relational* prefers to be by herself. She will work on projects alone and will probably have two or three very close friends. Those relationships will be deep and long lasting.[1]

How Do You Relate to Others?

The more we understand these qualities about ourselves the better we will function together to build up one another in the Lord. Finding which group fits you best will help you determine the type of service in which you will succeed.

If you prefer to work alone and have only one or two close friends, then being a greeter in the church foyer may prove extremely stressful for you. So would canvassing a new neighborhood for potential new members. Meeting a constant flow of unfamiliar people can be very threatening to your comfort zone.

---

[1] Multi-relational/ Familiar Group Relational/ and Singular Relational talents are copyrighted as a grouping of relational talents by the IDAK Group. Permission for use must be requested in writing.

What Part Do Circumstances Play?

Age, physical ability, and current circumstances all determine how and where you use the spiritual gifts God has given you. The focus of a young mother will differ greatly from that of the career woman or an elderly lady in a nursing home.

Kim, a young mother, spends her time caring for her husband and two small children, helping in the family business, and teaching a children's Sunday school class.

How different is the focus of Norma. She is a dietitian in a local hospital. Her hours are filled with meeting the needs of patients. In her spare time she teaches a nutrition class and is involved in the Career Class activities in her church.

Unlike either of them is Grandma Haynes, who lives in a retirement home for active seniors. This elderly woman spends her days visiting with the other "inmates" (her nickname for those who live in the home). She listens to their woes, helps them in the dining room, and teaches a Bible class. Grandma Haynes, in her current circumstances, is allowing God to use the gifts He has placed within her.

All three of these women are using their spiritual gifts, yet each has a completely different focus.

Are you confined to a wheelchair or lying flat in bed, frustrated because you can't go somewhere as a missionary? Look at the mission field opportunities right where you are. God has provided a unique set of circumstances that will allow you to display His gifts to the world around *you*.

Don't think that age, physical ability, or circumstances limit the use of your spiritual gifts. Instead, follow the Apostle Paul's admonition to young Timothy: "Do not neglect the spiritual gift within you" (1 Tim. 4:14, NASB).

Expand your vision, explore new opportunities, and allow God to be seen in you wherever you are.

Imbedded within you are all the gifts you need for your circumstances. Like tiny timed capsules, they'll be released exactly when needed and in the right quantity according to God's purpose.

Get to Know Yourself

1. List some of your learned skills (sewing, music, teaching, typing, counseling, etc.).
2. Try to describe your current circumstances (include age and physical abilities) to help you focus on your area of ministry.
3. What are you doing daily to improve your relationship with Jesus? (Daily prayer, Bible study, etc.)
4. During this week, what new avenue can you explore to allow God's gifts to be revealed through you?
5. Which of the three categories of relating fits you best? (Multi-relational, Familiar Group, or Singular Relational)

THE LEADING EDGE

CHAPTER THREE

"You'd make a great top sergeant!" my youngest brother says. He likes to tease me about always giving orders. And he is right. If I see a job that needs to be done, I immediately start telling people how to get it done. Or, if they are already doing it, I'll look for a way to do it more efficiently.

I was once introduced to the governor of Washington State as "Miss Efficiency" by my seventh-grade teacher. My teacher had given me that nickname when I cleaned up his messy desk. Twenty years later he remembered the nickname when he couldn't recall my actual name.

"I came—I saw—I made sure it got done" is the administrator's motto. That's what an administrator does. She gets the job done.

Biblical Definition

In the list of spiritual gifts in Rom. 12:8 the word *ruleth* (KJV) or *leadership* (NIV) really means, "the one who stands before, or the one who presides or rules." The definition also includes "to appoint, to establish, to continue."

In 1 Cor. 12:28 Paul uses the word *administration* (NIV) or *governments* (KJV), which means "steering," "pilotage" (as in the pilot of a ship), or "directorship."

God intends that this gift of ruling or administrating be used, not with an iron hand, but to see that all the jobs are actually accomplished. Jesus' great commission was, "Go and make disciples of all nations" (Matt. 28:19). He gave us an overwhelming job to do.

In order to accomplish that task somebody needs to see the overall goal and deploy the people to be sure all areas are covered. Someone needs to make sure there are ways and means of sending the people out and keeping them on the front lines. That's why God gave the gift of administration. It takes a commander or pilot to see that the job gets done and that people don't quit before it's finished.

Proverbs' Famous Lady Administrator

If ever there was a woman who demonstrated the attributes of an administrator, it's the Proverbs 31 woman. Read verses 10 through 31 of that chapter, and follow along with these comments (based on the New International Version).

(v. 13) She is a hard worker and cares about detail.

(vv. 14–15) She gets up before dawn and procures imported food for her family.

(v. 16) She is super-industrious. She knows about real estate values, buys land, and plants it. This isn't a grape arbor over the back porch; we're talking about serious crop farming.

(v. 17) Her work isn't all mental. She keeps physically fit and gets personally involved in her tasks.

(v. 18) She is a businesswoman. She sees to it that her business is profitable—so profitable, in fact, that she can burn oil all night long. No scrimping for this family!

(v. 19) Business isn't her only forte. She likes needlework. Although she has servants, she still isn't afraid of hard work. She does her own spinning personally.

(v. 20) Her family isn't her only concern. She reaches out to the needy people in her community. Charity is all in a day's work for her—just part of God's plan.

(vv. 21–22) Winter holds no fears for her family. She has made warm blankets and provided beautiful clothes for them and for herself. (Notice, she isn't dowdy!)

(v. 23) All the things she does enhance her husband's life. No one pities him because of a lazy, slovenly wife. (I'll bet a couple of those guys sitting with him at the city gates wish they'd been smart enough to marry her before he did!)

(v. 24) More business ventures pay off for her. First it was real estate and farming. Now it's clothing. She takes advantage of every opportunity.

(v. 25) There's no fear of the future for her. With all of her hard work, this family is secure.

(v. 26) She is a teacher. She shares her knowledge and is careful to only pass on the truth. Her students can trust what she teaches.

(v. 27) She supervises her household well and isn't idle.

(vv. 28–29) She well deserves all the praise she receives from her husband and children.

(v. 30) Her greatest attribute is that she fears the Lord. God is first and foremost in her life.

(v.31) With all of these characteristics, she has earned the praise of her community, too.

My Friend, the Administrator

My friend Joyce is a college math professor, and the students think so highly of her that her classes are bulging. Many have to be turned away. But her work doesn't stop there. She is the choir director for her church and sings in a mixed ensemble. She can also be found stripping the wallpaper in her living room, doing cross-stitch Christmas presents, or tutoring a junior high kid who needs help in math.

Joyce and her husband work together in Young Life (a Christian club for high schoolers), lead a marriage enrichment program, and often take teenagers on trips to the mountains or beach.

Because she works hard and adds to the family income, her family can spend vacations at a mountain lake cabin or once in a while fly to Hawaii. Joyce can be found backpacking in an extinct volcano, camping in a tent in the Oregon mountains, or kidnapping her husband for a surprise weekend in northern Washington. She makes superb spaghetti dinners, and her broccoli-cheese dish makes me sit up and beg. (And, I don't like broccoli!)

In all of this, Joyce puts Jesus first. If you need someone to pray with you about a problem, Joyce is the one to call. She is a vital, growing Christian who loves God above everything.

Sound too good to be true? Well, she's human just like the rest of us; there are some things she can't do. She has little patience with interruptions, wishy-washy people irritate her, and the tender care needed in the church nursery drives her up a wall. She willingly admits a lack of mercy gifts.

Like the Proverbs 31 woman, Joyce has the gift of administration and keeps her fingers in so many pies it's difficult for others to keep track of them all. God has gifted her and others like her with the ability to think and move in high gear. Not everyone is able to live with the high stress level of most administrators. But once in a while, even high stress people come to a screeching halt and have to put everything on hold while they rest.

Biblical Examples

There are also examples of administrators in the Bible. The Apostle Paul needed an administrator. He says in Titus 1:5, "The reason I left you [Titus] in Crete was that you might straighten out what was left unfinished and appoint elders in every town, as I directed you." All Paul had to say was, "Straighten out the mess." Apparently he knew Titus well enough that he could trust him to work out the details.

Titus must have demonstrated the abilities of administration. That's why Paul asked him to appoint elders in each town. Titus could easily see Paul's overall goal and quickly take the necessary, detailed steps to get the job done.

The early church spread rapidly and could have become chaotic if there hadn't been proper organization. Someone needed to be in charge of each church to keep it pure. Those overseers had to have specific standards, or the new Christians, like a mass of tiny kingdoms, would have followed the whims of each petty king, and the wholeness of the Christian Church would have been lost.

In ancient biblical times, Moses was wearing himself out trying to do everything alone. His father-in-law, Jethro, shows all the signs of a good administrator. He saw that Moses needed to delegate some of his jobs.

"Listen now to me and I will give you some advice," Jethro confronted Moses. "Select capable men . . . and appoint them as officials over thousands, hundreds, fifties and tens. . . . If you do this and God so commands, you will be able to stand the strain" (Ex. 18:19–27).

Jethro the administrator saw the problem and knew how to solve it. There was a more efficient way to judge the people. He divided up Moses' obligations into orderly chunks, pidgeon-holed each person's responsibility, and waited for Moses to react.

Sure enough, when Moses followed the steps of the organized plan, order emerged out of chaos. An overwhelming burden dissolved into an easy-flowing enterprise. Dusting off his hands in satisfaction, Jethro went home, another goal reached. "I came, I saw, I made sure it got done."

Moses was a great leader but he lacked administrative skills. God gave him a gifted administrator to complement and enhance his ministry.

Joys and Cautions

Every gift has its characteristic joys and cautions. Both will help us to identify the administrators and to understand them better. If you are an administrator, you can use this list to learn about yourself. The joys section will help you focus on the things you do well, and the cautions section can help you soften any possible negative impact you may have on people.

We need to know the caution side of our personalities as well as the joys. Yet, because we are Christians, we don't have to allow this caution side to dominate our lives. We can pray about these characteristics and yield them to God. Through the power of the Holy Spirit, they can be softened and controlled.

There are specific traits that help us identify those gifted with the ministry of administration. Let's examine them.

Characteristic Joys

1. She has the ability to perceive and set long-range goals and make specific plans to achieve them.

2. She is an organizer. She can take a series of tasks, organize them properly, and help others get organized, too.

3. She can take a large job and easily break it down into minute detail in order to reach the specific goal.

4. She can coordinate people and things (whatever it takes) to accomplish that goal.

5. She easily delegates responsibility and jobs to other people.

6. She considers pressure a friend; pressure helps get the job done.

7. She usually strives to accomplish her tasks ahead of schedule.

Characteristic Cautions

1. She pushes so hard to reach her goals that she may wear out other people involved.

2. She may seem to use people in order to get a project done; the project appears more important than people.

3. She doesn't seem to be sensitive to other people; she doesn't see their hurts until others mention the subject.

4. She responds to people in the same manner as they treat her.

5. Some people may perceive her as lazy because she tells others what to do rather than doing the job herself.

6. She can be bossy and overbearing.

7. She is nit-picky about any job.

Do you know someone like that? Have I described someone you know? Maybe it's you. Take a few moments to reflect on the people you know who fit this description. Can you see where knowing these things about her may help you to get along better?

If I've described you, can you see where you need to soften your approach with other people? You may already know some of these things about yourself, but it helps to see them printed on paper.

Getting Things Done

Nancy is another administrator. When she gets up in the morning, she immediately checks her list of things to do and arranges them according to priorities. Her closet is organized according to clothing types (skirts, slacks, blouses, sweaters, dresses) and subdivided by color. She is chairman of the women's group at church and president of a local service organization.

Nancy's family lives by *her* schedule. Dentist appointments, piano lessons, and football practice are all timed and coordinated carefully.

Her husband, on the other hand, isn't an administrator. He likes to take a vacation by just jumping in the car and seeing where they end up. He likes nothing better than to wander down the road and plan as they go. That type of attitude makes Nancy nervous. She needs to know where they are going, when they will get there, what they will do when they arrive, and how long they'll stay.

But the important thing about Nancy is that she gets things done. The church wanted to set up some type of program for helping those who were truly needy in their community. People were willing to give whatever was necessary, but nothing seemed to work out right. Donated items piled up in crumpled paper bags in a corner of the church basement, but there they stayed. Eventually the church women asked Nancy to head the program.

The first thing she did was to organize volunteers to search out needy families. She contacted individuals who were willing to donate food, clothing, services, or time, and found a room to use for the project headquarters. Today, that project is successful, providing aid to the needy and a sense of satisfaction to those who are helping.

Administrators are necessary to the body of Christ. If we didn't have them, many projects would bog down, and great ideas would never get off the ground.

There's nothing an administrator likes more than to be given a set of facts and figures that all pertain to one project. In no time at all she can mesh those facts and figures into a logical plan that, if followed, will most efficiently bring the project to completion.

Scripture not only identifies the gift of administration (ruler) but tells that person *how* to serve in that capacity. Rom. 12:8 says, "If [the gift] is leadership, let him govern diligently." Diligence carries the meaning of "careful speed, haste with a business attitude." What an unusual combination. The administrator is to be eager and quick, yet earnest and calculating. How wise of God to put that combination together.

If a person merely had to do a job quickly, then it might not be done well. The quality would suffer. Our God is quality conscious. He wants nothing but the best for the body of Christ.

On the other hand, if a person attacked a job only from the business point of view, it might take forever to complete even the smallest task. The person in charge might take so long to calculate all the tiny details that the job would never get done.

Reminders About the Gift of Administration

1. Don't confuse the administrator with the natural leader. An administrator is not usually a "people person." Natural leaders are likeable and nice to be around. People just seem to follow them. (Remember Moses?) They have fun ideas and a lot of enthusiasm, but they often lack administrative qualities. If an administrator is wise, she will work closely with a natural leader and let the natural leader be the buffer between committee members and her own more businesslike personality.

2. An administrator can easily become overworked. Because she is known for getting the job done, she is dumped with "just one more" job in her lap. People know she can juggle jobs like circus clowns juggle oranges. Although pressure is her friend, and she works well with a deadline, too many jobs will burn her out. They will take their toll on her life. Her family and health may suffer unless she paces herself carefully.

3. Not every woman with a well-organized life has the gift of administration. Many of us have either *learned* organizational skills or our lifestyles have required us to *adapt* to some administrative roles. For example, if you have a busy family, you've learned to schedule appointments and see that the children complete their homework. If you've been involved in church work for a number of years, you probably have had to organize a project or head a committee. Just because you've filled the role of an administrator doesn't mean you have that gift.

I once asked a group of women how many thought they had the gift of administration. To my surprise *all* of those women thought administration was their gift. It wasn't until we analyzed their lifestyles that we learned why. They were all normal, busy women with jobs, families, and church activities. They had all filled chairmanship roles and juggled schedules so that everything got done. If you are a wife and mother in today's world, you probably have to demonstrate some administrative skills just to survive. But there is a difference between the learned skill and the gift.

Joan and Sherry each held an administrative position in a Bible class. When she began her term, Joan received a box containing all sorts of papers that related to the class. There were blank forms, instruction sheets, and piles of other related items. Joan glanced at them and, for the most part, left them alone. Once in a while, if she needed something, she pawed through the box and found the item.

When her term of service ended, she handed the box to Sherry. The next week Joan was amazed to see everything out of the box and organized into neat folders. Sherry had labeled, sorted, and arranged them for their most efficient use.

Joan and Sherry both held the title of administrator, but there the similarity ended. Although Joan learned her job and accomplished what she had been told to do, she didn't have the gift of administration. Sherry, on the other hand, demonstrated in the first week on the job some of the characteristics of the administration gift. Her ability was not learned. Rather, it was a natural expression of the personality God had given her.

If You Score Low in Administration

If, after you complete the Discovery Evaluation in Chapter 10, you find you are quite low in the area of administration, you might consider the following: Agree to work on a committee, but allow someone else to be the chairperson. Sing in the choir, but allow someone else to be the director. Work in the Sunday school, but don't be the program director or supervisor.

If You Score High in Administration

If you score extremely high in administration, you might avoid working directly with the elderly or very young children. Those two areas require a very sensitive person, and many administrators often unintentionally come across as insensitive, harsh, and critical.

Actually, for me it was a relief not to have to work with children. Because I know my area of service is mainly administration, I no longer feel guilty when I say no to teaching a children's Sunday school class. Does that absolve me of all responsibility? Of course not! An administrator can still be a class secretary, a general program director (supervisor), or overseer of the resource room.

Varying Approaches

Each of us can be involved in the same area but approach the work differently according to our particular gifts. For example, let's say a certain Sunday school had a large class of primary children. In order to keep the class functioning, the church decided to ask a different person to help each week. Here's how the people approached the job:

Encouraging quickly gathered the children around her and concentrated on memorizing Scripture verses with them.

Mercy held the children in her lap and kissed their

skinned knees, paying special attention to a handicapped child.

After class, *Administration* placed the chairs in precise rows, reorganized the supplies cabinet, and created a more efficient attendance record book.

Giving spent her time deciding how many new tables and chairs the room needed and calculated the cost of a new carpet and paint job, quietly making plans to pay for it herself.

Serving kept the children supplied with crayons and paper, noted two children who needed new shoes, and made arrangements with *Giving* to help paint the room on Saturday.

Teaching took a small group of children to one corner of the room after their lesson and helped them apply the Bible story to their own lives.

Prophecy knelt beside the chair of one child who really had a question about sin. She carefully explained the difference between right and wrong.

We can all handle the same job; we'll just approach it from the viewpoint of our individual gifts. Our involvement will vary according to the way God embroidered our lives.

So what do you do if you find yourself chairman of a committee and administration really isn't high on your list of gifts? Begin by looking at the gifts God has given to you. Determine how you can use those gifts in this situation. Then enlist the help of someone who obviously has administrative qualities. Ask for guidelines and use them. Realize that you will approach your task from the perspective of your own gifts.

There are a number of books written on how to lead a meeting. Take advantage of this skill-building opportunity and seek out the help of experts.

You may not handle the job the same way that a gifted administrator might, but you'll do it to the best of your ability with God's help. In fact, you may be surprised at how well the job gets done when you turn it over to God and allow Him to work through you.

When you are placed in a position of leadership, remember you aren't "the boss" but you are God's servant. You aren't to dominate or rule with an iron hand. Your job is to coordinate, organize, and "pilot" the group. That means you'll take care of your ship, crew, and cargo as well as guide it to its destination.

When it's time to elect officials or board members, the church should look for those with the ministry of administration. Too often people are elected because of their popularity or because they have a natural charisma, or even worse, because they've held that position for twenty years! We do our church and the body of Christ a disservice when we allow those other things to influence our choices. Be diligent in your selection. Be sure there are *some* God-gifted administrators on the board.

Uses Today

In a nutshell, the person who has the gift of administration is one who can perceive long-range goals, and organize and implement effective plans to achieve those goals. How is this gift used today? You can make your own list, but here are some ideas to help you get started:

Planning future projects
Leading meetings
Controlling discipline, keeping order
Serving on committees, boards
Directing organizations or ministries

Serving in executive positions
Doing secretarial work

Exploring the Possibilities

How do you explore the possibility that you may have the gift of administration? First, of course, pray and ask God's wisdom. In fact, you should do that constantly as you are reading this book.

If you think this chapter somewhat describes you, be willing to accept some responsibility in the area of administration. Don't hold back because you think someone else would do it better. Allow God to work through you. Offer to assist your Sunday school superintendent. Ask to help in the church office. Be available to serve on a committee or even lead it.

Promises to Claim

"The elders who direct the affairs of the church well are worthy of double honor" (1 Tim. 5:17).

"If any of you lacks wisdom, he should ask God, who gives generously to all without finding fault, and it will be given to him" (James 1:5).

For Further Study

Titus 1:5–9; 1 Tim. 3:1–7; 1 Pet. 5:2–3; 1 Thess. 5:12–13; Heb. 13:7, 17; Mark 10:42–44.

Questions to Ponder

Think back over the last few times you were chairman of a committee, in charge of a meeting or program, or involved in a long-term project. Evaluate how you functioned:

1. Did you accomplish your goals easily and quickly?
2. Were other people pleased with your work? Did they ask you to take on another similar job?
3. How did you feel about what you did?
4. Has God repeatedly placed administrative opportunities in your path? Is He offering one to you right now?

AN APPLE FOR THE TEACHER

CHAPTER FOUR

"Dixie, I don't know which form of the verb to use in this situation; can you help me?" I was talking on the phone with my friend, an English professor at a local college. I was in a hurry and a word had me absolutely stumped. All I wanted from her was a quick answer.

But true to her calling, Dixie took her time, forcing me to think through the rules and eventually make my own decision. Believe me, I have never forgotten that word or how to use it. She caused me to learn.

Dixie is more than a gifted English teacher. She also uses her gift to minister to the body of Christ. In her classes I have learned a depth about the Bible I never knew was there. She challenged me to study, to seek information on my own outside the classroom. She made it fun to learn, even when the concepts were difficult.

God uses teachers to communicate His truth to us. If left to ourselves, most of us would do little more than scratch the surface of His Word. Teachers cause us to learn what we need to know about God.

Biblical Definition

"If it is teaching, let him teach" (Rom. 12:7). What exactly does this word *teaching* mean? The Greek word used in this verse is *didasko*, which means to teach in a way that causes others to learn. This is the same word used to describe the way Jesus taught while on earth.

When the chief priests and teachers of the law tried to entrap Jesus (Luke 20:21–26), He used His gifts as a teacher to impart a heavenly concept to them. "Give to Caesar what is Caesar's, and to God what is God's." This was a new truth to them, and they were astonished. But Jesus did more than give them a new truth. He presented the material in such a unique way that they would never forget it.

Besides confronting the learned men of His day, Jesus taught anyone who came to hear Him. "Each day Jesus was teaching at the temple" (Luke 21:37). He communicated God's truth to all who wanted to learn. (Also read Luke 5:17; Matt. 4:23; 9:35; 21:23; 26:55.)

The word *teaching* carries with it the meaning of "weight." The teacher bears a heavy responsibility to be sure others learn the knowledge she has. She is responsible to search out the truth about that knowledge, to be sure it is absolutely accurate so that any information she passes on to the pupil is true.

The ministry of teaching then is twofold: accuracy and communication. The teacher is always questioning facts and information: Is this fact true? Is this information accurate? The teacher is also burdened by the necessity of clearly communicating truthful information to others.

Biblical Example

Philip was that kind of teacher. Jesus had just explained to the disciples that He was about to go to heaven and prepare a place for them. Thomas didn't understand and asked, "How can we know the way?"

Jesus replied, "I am the way and the truth and the life. No one comes to the Father except through me. If you really knew me, you would know my Father as well. From now on, you do know him and have seen him" (John 14:5–7).

That was a lot of new information for Philip to digest, and he wanted to check it out. Searching for truth and accuracy, Philip said, "Lord, show us the Father and that will be enough for us" (v. 8).

His motive for asking wasn't unbelief. He had a burning desire to know the truth, a trait typical of one who ministers through teaching. Later, Philip displays in a more obvious way the ministry to which he had been called.

In obedience to God's guidance, Philip was traveling on the desert road that led from Jerusalem to Gaza. Along the way he met an Ethiopian eunuch who was reading from the book of Isaiah. "Do you understand what you are reading?" Philip asked. (Notice the teacher traits in him?) "Then Philip began with that very passage of scripture and told him the good news about Jesus" (Acts 8:30, 35).

Apparently, he explained the scripture so thoroughly that the eunuch understood it, because the man immediately took action. That's real teaching: life-changing information communicated in a heart-comprehended manner. When a teacher reaches the heart of the pupil and causes the pupil to act on the new information, then learning has occurred.

Acquired Skill or Spiritual Gift?

Not every person who acts in the position of a teacher has the ability to reach the student's heart. Anyone can learn how to take in information and pass it on. In fact, I've attended Bible classes under a few teachers like that. They probably glanced at the prepackaged teacher's lesson on Saturday night and parroted it on Sunday morning exactly as it was written. There wasn't much real teaching going on. They simply passed along information.

There is a difference between the learned skill of teaching that can be acquired through a college degree program and the spiritual gift of teaching. The first is available to anyone who is diligent in school. The second is the result of the Holy Spirit working through the teacher to build up the body of Christ.

Lori knows she isn't a teacher. She often uses words incorrectly. She doesn't bother to think of the right word if a similar-sounding one can get her general meaning across. Multiple sclerosis becomes mocopoco-nosis. If she tried to teach, her students would spend so much energy trying to guess what she meant that they wouldn't learn anything.

Tanya is a great storyteller and entertainer, but she isn't a teacher, either. Often, when she tells her stories, they don't relate to the subject. If she's joining a discussion on a biblical topic, the examples she uses are often inappropriate for the truth of the lesson.

Both of these ladies are nice people, but they are not gifted teachers. Neither of them displays the qualities of communicating God's truth in a way that causes the listener to learn.

What characteristics will you find in one who has the spiritual gift of teaching? As you read through this list, think about people you know with these traits. Evaluate yourself. How well do these statements describe you?

Characteristic Joys

1. She loves research and checking information, words, and their definitions.

2. She requires that words be used absolutely accurately.

3. She finds it easy to gather, organize and retain a large amount of facts.

4. She is a very logical person and is usually objective.

5. She demands to know the authority behind information and insists that illustrations be completely within context.

6. If there is a problem, she implements an appropriate teaching method rather than giving a simple solution.

7. She gives detailed instructions to others and presents her facts in a very systematic way.

8. She has a burning thirst for knowledge and always wants to know the *whys*.

9. She searches exhaustively for illustrations that will add meaning to her instruction.

Characteristic Cautions

With all her joys there are some characteristics a teacher needs to be cautious about. She can change these and soften them if she yields to the power of the Holy Spirit. Ask yourself, "If these things are true about me, how can I change them so I will more effectively serve Christ?"

1. Because she wants to correct any misinformation and is always asking *why*, she may appear to be overly critical.

2. Because she speaks in such detail, she may bore others.

3. Unless controlled, she can become prideful of her knowledge.

Randy is one of the body of Christ who has the ministry of teaching. She also has another gift. (Remember, our gifts are like a bouquet, and we have more than one flower.) The largest blossom in Randy's bouquet is named Teaching, but she has some flowers almost as big called Encouraging (exhortation). This woman chooses to use the combination of her gifts in teaching an adult Sunday school class. Randy spends hours and hours every week researching material for her class. She searches through five or six Bible translations, checking the meanings of words, and she studies about that same number of commentaries. Randy isn't satisfied to simply follow the Sunday school material she was given by her denomination. She hunts for current, vivid illustrations to clarify the main points of her lesson.

If her students ask questions in class, Randy either asks a question in return that will cause them to discover their own answer, or she'll go through a step-by-step explanation to make the material absolutely clear.

On her job, when Randy is presented with some new material, she never accepts it on face value. She'll do some checking on her own to prove its accuracy.

At home, when she tells her kids to do a job, they often get impatient because she explains her instructions in minute detail. She doesn't just tell her son to rake the leaves. She says, "Get the rake out of the garage and start in the back corner. Work toward the center. When that's done, get the garbage can and take it out to your pile of leaves and put them into it . . ."

If she tells her family about something that happened during the day, they sometimes get bored because she has to backtrack and tell all the tiny details.

But Randy loves to teach. Not long ago her pastor wanted to add a night class for Sunday-school teachers on how to be more effective in teaching. Randy plunged in as the instructor and found many innovative teaching methods to share. The class has been very successful.

Incidentally, Randy's husband is not gifted as a teacher, but he shares in his wife's ministry by relieving her of some of her evening tasks so that she can have more study time.

The Importance of the Teaching Gift

Why is this gift necessary to the body of Christ? What makes it important enough to be included in the list of things God wants His people to be doing? First, biblical truth must be preserved and maintained. Second, biblical truth must be communicated accurately.

Without the ministry of teaching, biblical truths would lose accuracy and fade into mythical stories, violated at the whim of the storyteller's imagination. The hearers might become so bored that they wouldn't listen or be encouraged to make any life-changing decisions.

Five women who wanted to be taught the Scriptures approached a missionary and asked her to lead a Bible study. The missionary had recently returned from China and seemed the logical choice as their teacher. This plain, statuesque English lady, who bore a strong resemblance to George Washington, agreed to teach them, but warned that she would not spoon-feed anyone. The students would have to dig into scriptural truth according to her instructions.

Miss A. Weatherall Johnson had no idea she was starting an international Bible study group with these five women. Miss J., as she became affectionately known, created a clear, comprehensive method for studying Scripture that has ministered to thousands and thousands of people around the world. Bible Study Fellowship began with one woman's obedience to God, allowing Him to use her spiritual gift of teaching.

Through the power of the Holy Spirit, Miss Johnson was able to communicate accurate spiritual truths in such a manner that the student thoroughly learned the material. The method is so clear that it allows a student of any level to learn and be challenged. But it doesn't stop there. Miss J. also created a method for raising up new leaders who could follow in her steps to multiply the spiritual fruit of Bible study.

Through all of this, Miss Johnson kept her purpose clear. She wanted only to present Christ and His truth. The body of Christ needs more gifted teachers who are willing to be used by the Holy Spirit to reach others with biblical truth.

If You Score Low in Teaching

If you score very low in teaching, you may wish to allow someone else to be the teacher while you fill a supportive role. There are any number of things a nonteacher can do that will help the teacher in his or her job. Try to find a supportive area that utilizes your strongest gifts.

Some obvious support areas are: doing secretarial work for a class, decorating the classroom, organizing social activities for the class, helping with handwork, and calling on absentees. Ask the teacher what needs to be done.

If You Score High in Teaching

If you score quite high, you may become frustrated sitting under a less-than-accurate instructor. Choose the classes you attend carefully. With teacher traits yourself, you may scrutinize your instructor more closely than others will.

You may also find yourself frustrated by being in a nonteaching situation. Prayerfully consider exactly how God wants you to use His gift to build up the body of Christ. Your frustration may be a signal that you should offer to teach a class.

Just a note of caution: if you offer to teach a class, have some nitroglycerin tablets handy in case the supervisor or pastor has a heart attack. People don't often *offer* to teach a class!

Varying Approaches

If you have the ministry of teaching, look to see how it blends with your other spiritual gifts. For example, if you have a teacher/administration mix, you'll want to work with adults and will probably present your material in a more factual manner. If you have a teaching/mercy blend, you'd do very well with the elderly or young children. A person with a teaching/encouraging combination will communicate biblical truth, focusing on encouraging applications for her pupils.

Remember, each gifted person will approach the task of teaching differently according to the blend of the spiritual gifts she has been given. Also, each teacher communicates more comfortably in a certain size group. You may discover that you teach better in a one-on-one situation, or a small group. Or, you may learn that you can relax more teaching a large group.

Writing is one of the most comfortable ways for me to teach. What God causes me to learn through experience, I can then teach others through articles, books, and stories. The learned skill of putting words on paper is an excellent avenue for building up the body of Christ.

Think about which area is most comfortable for you and write it at the end of this chapter. This may become important as you explore new ways to use the gift of teaching.

What do you do if you've discovered that teaching isn't your gift, and you have to teach anyway? Let's assume that you are in a small church, and you're already teaching a class. Do you immediately resign? Of course not.

Just approach that position in light of your own gifts. At the moment, the gifts *you* have may be more necessary than the teaching gift. Someone in that class may need exactly what you have to offer.

But determine what other gifts need to be at work in your class to make it complete. Then ask for help from people who have the gifts you are lacking. Together you can meet the needs of the body of Christ in the spot where He has placed you.

What if you aren't teaching a class and the supervisor asks you to take on the responsibility of teaching. How do you answer? Do you say that's not your gift and ask her to find someone else? Perhaps you could pray about it first. God may be stretching you, asking you to explore a new area of service. Be sure you are following God's direction when you answer yes or no.

Can All Believers Be Teachers?

Early Christians were expected to reach others with the gospel. "By this time you ought to be teachers," says Heb. 5:12. "Each one teach one" was a natural creed. They were to share what they had learned. The need was (and still is) so great that every believer had the responsibility to pass along the good news about Jesus.

But do all believers have the gift of teaching? In his first letter to the Corinthians, Paul confronted them with the knowledge of the body of Christ. He told them that God had appointed people in the church to function in different capacities. But then he asked the question, "Are all apostles? Are all prophets? Are all teachers? Do all work miracles?" (1 Cor. 12:29). The implication is that not everyone has the God-appointed gift of teaching.

Uses Today

Capsulized, *teaching* is the ability to research and communicate information in such a way that others will learn and the body of Christ will be built up.

As you read through the following list, write in some thoughts of your own.

Teaching Sunday school
Pastoring
Instructing in Christian education
Developing Christian education materials
Discipling (one-on-one or class situation)
Teaching a Bible study
Speaking
Writing
Acting/directing drama
Singing

Exploring the Possibilities

Has God been nudging you to get involved as a teacher? Consider leading a private Bible study group, perhaps in a unique situation rather than the traditional Sunday school class. A neighborhood Bible study or teen group is a good place to start. Or maybe God is prompting you to reach an otherwise forgotten group (nursing home residents? ethnic group? handicapped?). Be open to the leading of the Holy Spirit.

If music is your skill, carefully choose songs that teach biblical truths.

Recently I was privileged to attend a concert given by a Christian college group. Not only was their concert entertaining and uplifting but they presented a song that truly touched our hearts with scriptural truth. One song included a bit of drama that moved me emotionally and caused me to see a truth God had been trying to tell me for quite some time. I came away from the concert confronted by God.

This was a good demonstration of the teaching gift combined with drama/music skills.

As you explore, seek also to increase your skills by new and updated training. Take classes at a nearby college in speaking, communicating, teaching methods, music, or drama. Enhance whatever natural talents God has given you so that your areas of ministry can increase.

Promises to Claim

"Therefore every teacher of the law who has been instructed about the kingdom of heaven is like the owner of a house who brings out of his storeroom new treasures as well as old" (Matt. 13:52).

"I will instruct you and teach you in the way you should go; I will counsel you and watch over you" (Ps. 32:8).

"Instruct a wise man and he will be wiser still; teach a righteous man and he will add to his learning" (Prov. 9:9).

"But the Counselor, the Holy Spirit, whom the Father will send in my name, will teach you all things and will remind you of everything I have said to you" (John 14:26).

For Further Study

1 Cor. 12:28; Eph. 4:11–14; James 3:1; Rom. 12:7; Acts 18:24–28; Acts 20:20–21; 1 Tim. 1:3–4; 4:16; 2 Tim. 2:24–26; 3:15–17; 4:2–3; Titus 1:9–16.

Questions to Ponder

1. What size audience did you discover to be the most comfortable for you (one-on-one, small group, large group)?
2. If you are already involved in a teaching situation, with what type of audience are you most comfortable (young children, teens, young adults, mixed audience, senior adults, other)?
3. As a teacher, do you easily accept other people's material or do you research it yourself, often adding more information?
4. Have you often been encouraged to continue in your teaching capacity? How many of your pupils (audience) have honestly said you have helped them to make important life changes? Make a list of those people and what they said. (Limit your list to incidents during the past six months.)
5. If God is speaking to you about some type of teaching ministry, what is it? Remember it could be speaking, music, drama, writing (e.g., books, stories, articles, lesson materials), or some other form of teaching.

ENCOURAGE ONE
ANOTHER

CHAPTER FIVE

The hospital room was small and crowded with equipment. Matching tears welled up in Debi's eyes as she watched the patient trying in vain to control the tears that dampened her cheeks. Cancer and surgery complications had nearly taken the woman's life, and now six weeks of struggling had left its battle scars.

For some unknown reason the patient couldn't eat more than one or two bites of food at a meal. "I try so hard," she told Debi, "but I can't do it! It would be so easy to just give up." Verbally she acknowledged that she needed to eat food in order to live, but something held her back. "I'm so discouraged," she added, attempting to wipe the tears with her emaciated hand.

"Lord," Debi prayed silently, "her family has tried to encourage her. She's been told the battle is over; she has won the surgical war. Now all she needs to do is eat to regain her strength. But nothing anyone says seems to reach her. Help me to use the skills and knowledge you've given me to bring her through this crisis."

Debi reached out and patted the limp hand. "I'm the hospital nutritionist, and I've come to tell you you're doing really great," she said. "You have no reason to be discouraged. After all you've been through, you are eating exactly the amount you should. You are trying to make your body ingest as much as you did before your illness. Quit trying so hard. Eat just a little bit and increase it slowly."

As they talked, the patient's tears subsided, then dried completely. Nearly forty-five minutes later Debi left the room, promising to bring a small tray of food. To see a plate with only a few bites of food, the amount the patient could easily eat, would make the woman feel as if she had accomplished a lot rather than being discouraged by seeing all the food she *wasn't* eating.

The next day Debi placed a chart on the wall showing how much food the patient had eaten compared to the amount of nutrition she was getting intravenously. In the days following, the red (food) columns grew and the blue (IV) columns shrank. In the course of a week the patient was eating normally and eventually left the hospital.

Debi is an encourager. Each person involved had tried to say something to help, but the gifted one had all the right words. Debi was using her gift to meet the needs of one of God's hurting lambs.

Biblical Definition

"If it is encouraging, let him encourage" (Rom. 12:8). Some translations use the term *exhortation*, but encouraging is a much better translation of the original meaning.

The actual word in the Greek is *parakaleo*, which means to call near, to invite, to comfort. This particular form of the word means "to call near," as in drawing near to the person. It also means to invite and to comfort, including spoken words. It isn't limited to spoken comfort, but it includes that meaning.

One of the words used in Scripture for the Holy Spirit is *Paraklete*. That comes from this same word. The Holy Spirit comes near and speaks to us in comfort and encouragement. So the person with the ministry of encouragement will serve in the same way.

In the last chapter we talked about the gift of teaching. The gift of encouraging goes beyond teaching information to the next step. The teacher may stand in front of the class and list the spiritual truths and principles that Christians are to follow, but the encourager will personally stand *beside* you. The encourager will urge you to take daily positive steps to implement the principles you learned from the teacher.

Biblical Examples

This same word is used to describe what John the Baptist did in the wilderness. "And with many other words John exhorted [*parakaleo*] the people" (Luke 3:18).

My childhood image of this story conjured up visions of John the Baptist preaching up a storm and shaking his fist at the world. But according to the word used, he was encouraging and urging the people to a better life, trying to show them the way.

According to the book of Acts, Peter, Paul, Barnabas, Silas, and Judas (who was called Barsabbas) all encouraged (*parakaleo*) others as they began to spread the gospel.

But the word is probably most used by Paul. He is described as *parakaleo* wherever he went—encouraging them in the faith, urging them to a better life, better deeds. When training Timothy in how to lead the people in his care, Paul uses the word *encourage*. Titus is told that this is an attribute required of an elder. And in Heb. 3:13 we are commanded to "encourage one another daily."

The ministry of encouragement is basically three-pronged: comfort, encouragement, and counsel. But it is all tied to scriptural application. The encourager will comfort according to God's Word. She will counsel along the lines of scriptural principles. She will encourage others to live lives according to God's plan as revealed in the Bible.

If you come to an encourager with a problem, she will not simply give you an answer. The encourager will look for a way to cause you to grow spiritually as well as help you to discover your own solution.

Have you ever seen somebody who is just a bump on a log spiritually? He or she has warmed the same spot on the same pew for who knows how long, and you never see any spiritual growth in them. You even wonder why they are still there. Show an encourager a spiritual "bump on a pew" and she will leap to the challenge. The encourager loves to urge people, including spiritual "bumps," to grow in their relationship with the Lord.

Having the dual gifts of teaching and encouragement, Jayne began teaching an adult Sunday school class. She was appalled, however, at how many of the members had been in that class for years, came week after week, and never studied a single lesson. Some even dozed off during class time.

In the weeks and months following, Jayne included challenges in her lessons that caused the class members to study at home. Within a year almost half of the class had moved out into areas of service, becoming involved in ministries they never dreamed they could do.

One of those women is a retired nurse with the gifts of mercy and encouragement. She is now working in a

Bible class for handicapped or slightly retarded children. This is a natural area for her to be involved in because usually the encourager works well with wayward, addicted, or handicapped people.

Read through these joys and cautions of an encourager prayerfully. Do they describe you? Do they describe someone you know?

Characteristic Joys

1. She thoroughly enjoys counseling other people.
2. She views problems as an opportunity for spiritual growth.
3. She is able to define positive steps to solving a problem or need.
4. She loves to make practical applications from Scripture to everyday life.
5. She has the ability to verbally comfort the hurting.
6. She enjoys challenging the spiritually apathetic to grow in the Lord.
7. She is usually consistent and dependable.
8. She enjoys being around other people.

Characteristic Cautions

1. Because the steps to spiritual growth are so clear to her, she may make the solution too simple.
2. Because she is interested in the essence rather than detail, she may take some things out of context in order to press a point.
3. Because she is so interested in seeing spiritual growth, she may be thought to be unfeeling.
4. She may be so motivated to success that she spends more time on working out a solution than the counselee does.

If you are an encourager, from time to time you may want to evaluate how much time and effort you are spending with a counselee. You probably have a tendency to overdo, and you may give them more than they want. Don't waste your time and energy. You need to keep a balance in your life. Beware of becoming so involved in your counselee's situation that you neglect your own life and/or your family.

More Identifying Traits

An encourager might say of herself, "I can see what people can become with God's help, and I want to help them do it. I hurt when others are hurting and I want to help them turn to God for their answers."

To help you identify encouragers, here are some things you might say about someone who has the ministry of encouraging:

"Whenever we visit I always come away feeling helped. I have some new goal to reach, whether it's large or small."

"She makes me feel good when I'm around her. She's so enthusiastic."

"Even if I've taken a nose-dive, she always encourages me to get up and try again."

"In her lesson she misquoted the words to that song, but the scriptural principle was there."

At a recent funeral I attended, the pastor misquoted the words to a song. I'm sure he didn't do it deliberately, but he missed a couple of words. Rather than dig out a copy of the song to get the actual words, he merely substituted some other words that conveyed the same message. It fit, it made the point, and no one was hurt by it. He was more concerned about encouraging the family and other mourners than he was about the accuracy of the words.

Last week I dashed into the church office to work on our annual ladies' retreat. Jan, the church secretary, greeted me with a broad smile, pointed to the copy machine, and nodded an OK as she continued talking on the phone. Holding the phone between her shoulder and her ear, she dug out her scissors for me with one hand while scribbling the phone message for the pastor with the other.

During the time I was there, several people called with messages of family illness. Jan's words of comfort poured over the telephone to ease their pain. Later, she paused beside me and asked, "How are you?"

Paper clips stuffed between my teeth, I mumbled "Fine" over the noise of the copy machine.

"No," she said, planting herself firmly in front of me. "I mean, how are *you*!" Her tone brooked no argument. She really cared and wanted to know exactly what was happening in my life. It wasn't the first time she had confronted me with her caring attitude. Jan regularly prays for me and, in love, won't accept a noncommittal "fine" answer from me.

Jan has the combined gifts of administration and encouragement. She finds her position of church secretary tailor-made for those gifts.

We all need encouragement. That's one of the main reasons this gift was given to the body of Christ. All believers need to be urged to live a better Christian life.

The body also needs comfort, words of healing, and counseling. We need to be challenged to grow spiritually. As we sit at the seat of learning, we need a practical interpretation of what the teacher is saying. New Christians especially need to hear how to apply the Word to their daily lives. All these are functions of the one gifted with encouragement.

If You Score Low in Encouraging

If you are *not* an encourager, you may wish to avoid in-depth, personal counseling situations and hospital or nursing home visits.

I was visiting a close friend in the hospital when a man came in to see the patient. Because Scripture says to "visit the sick," he came in and stood at the foot of the hospital bed. After a brief hello, with legs staunchly apart, arms folded across his chest, he glared silently at my friend. For several minutes I waited for the visitor to strike up a conversation, ask how the patient was feeling, or talk about the weather. But nothing happened. He stood in the same position, absolutely silent.

I made a couple attempts at conversation, but he only nodded. Finally I excused myself and went out to ask the nurse a question, thinking that perhaps the visitor had something personal he wanted to say to my friend. But when I came back, the situation hadn't changed. After about ten minutes, the man left.

With a twinkle in his eye, my friend turned to me and said, "That's the most difficult visitor I have. He comes once a month to see me whether I'm in the hospital or at the retirement home, and exactly the same thing happens. Sometimes he will stand there for as much as half an hour. I feel like he's waiting for me to die!"

It's taxing on the one being visited if the visitor isn't able to communicate well. We need to recognize that some of us do not have the gift of encouragement.

If You Score High in Encouraging

If you are an encourager, you may feel frustrated in a situation where you are not able to share scriptural truth. Perhaps your job is one where you must keep quiet about your beliefs. That's the way Raye feels. She works for a government agency and absolutely cannot bring up anything pertaining to her spiritual beliefs.

Time after time, Raye has been in situations in which she desperately wanted to tell a co-worker how much God could help her with a specific problem. But the rules keep her from offering the help needed. "There were two ladies in our office who were constantly bickering," she told me. "The original problem had been very small, but because it was never resolved, the women continued to plague one another until the tension in our office was as thick as cheesecake."

"I've tried all the normal avenues of reconciliation," Raye confided, "but each one needs to be willing to give up her own rights and yield her hurts to Christ." She sighed heavily, "Yet I can't say that or I'll be reported. It's really frustrating!"

I know of elementary schoolteachers who want to use the Christmas story for programs in December, and high school science teachers who want to include the biblical account of creation to help combat evolution. Yet, because of the laws of our land, these people are frustrated, unable to share their spiritual beliefs in their daily world of work.

The encourager may also see the details of administration as unnecessary and boring.

Ron and Joyce attended a class I was teaching on this subject, and when I made the above statement, Ron nodded in agreement while his wife laughed. "Now, you're talking!" Ron exclaimed.

Joyce is a college math teacher and is gifted as an administrator, while Ron is a teacher/encourager. "She gets so nit-picky about details—down to the penny on the checkbook, and our social calendar is scheduled for months ahead! I really think all that stuff is boring."

"That's true," Joyce nodded. "He doesn't want to

know the details. He leaves them all to me. Your statements about an encourager really describe Ron."

Another attribute of an encourager is that she may not be satisfied with a clinical approach. "Writing out a check to meet a need isn't satisfying," Anne said. "I'd rather talk with the one in need and help her find her own solution to the problem."

Varying Approaches

Through his travels across the country, author Lee Roddy became aware that many people (including Christians) are in silent pain. He says, "They prove Thoreau's contention that the mass of men lead lives of quiet desperation."

Mr. Roddy decided to do something, no matter how small it was, to demonstrate God's love to those hurting people. "The Barnabas Group resulted," he says. "My goal was to write one person a day and let them know I cared or was thinking of them. If I missed a day, I made it up with two letters a day. I asked each person if I could pray specifically for a need he or she had."

People wrote back and told him how "coincidentally" his letters arrived at a time when they needed some encouragement. Their response was so encouraging to Mr. Roddy that he decided to expand his concept. So, he began inviting others to do something similar.

"A note from you today to somebody about whom you care may be worth more than you can guess," he writes. "Show someone you care. Somebody needs to hear from you today!"[2]

As I mentioned this idea in one of my spiritual gifts classes, Martha suddenly snapped to attention. For sev-

---

[2]For more information about The Barnabas Group contact: Lee Roddy, P.O. Box 700, Penn Valley, CA 95946.

eral weeks she had been sitting quietly while we discussed spiritual gifts and how they could be used. One by one, the others in the class were beginning to identify their gifts and possible applications, yet Martha had remained unmoved.

"If you can't do anything else for someone who is hurting," I told the class, "write them a note of encouragement." Martha sat taller in her chair and began writing furiously in her notebook. Her eyes sparkled, and she drank in every word we said during that part of the discussion.

Later, I received the first of several notes from her. In it she explained that she didn't feel comfortable approaching others in person, yet she really cared how they felt. "I'll be praying for you as you finish teaching this series of classes," she added.

Over the next few weeks I heard from other people who had received notes from Martha. All told me how meaningful those notes were.

Quiet Martha, who thought she had no gifts or talents, had found a way to serve Christ through encouraging others.

One form of encouragement we often overlook is humor. Sometimes a joke or something funny can be a great form of encouragement to a person under stress.

Recently I found myself under some extra strain. With all of our commitments, business pressures, family stress, and the illness of a close family member, my husband and I felt overwhelmed. There weren't enough hours in the day to keep up with our obligations, let alone get anything accomplished.

One morning I brought in the mail and tossed it on my desk, intending to open only the "important" things and leave the rest until later. But one envelope caught my eye. I didn't recognize the return address and there was no name. Ripping it open, I discovered a single sheet of paper folded inside. On it were only a series of numbers, no writing or explanation.

25 1320,
    1992 4012 3874
(pp)1261 1336 4336 (pp)1247 (pp)1340.
700 4336 (pp)1247 (pp)1273, 2532.

26,
1249

Intrigued, I completely forgot all the "important" things that were pressuring me. What could it mean? The puzzle twisted through my mind while I fixed a cup of tea. By the time the brew was just right an idea materialized. I pulled a Bible concordance off the shelf and turned to the section of numbered Greek words. Sure enough, the first word I looked up made sense. Very quickly the message became clear except for the ones marked (pp). When I realized those were page numbers, the message finally emerged:

Dear Teacher,
    Letter regarding comfort
I continually pray to God earnestly for you.
Please pray to God earnestly for me, too.

Love,
Servant

Now I knew who had written the letter. Roy, my friend's husband, had been a student in one of my classes. I often stressed the importance of looking up the meanings of words and encouraged the use of Bible concordances in their study. Roy and his wife had been supporting me in prayer, and as an encourager with a very dry wit, he chose this unique form of encouragement.

Those few minutes spent deciphering his message were like a vacation for me. I chuckled all day while I went through my normal business. Every once in a while I'd share his note with someone and we'd all laugh. Humor had broken the tension, and as I relaxed, the strain eased. Encouragement is one of God's best medicines in a stress-filled world.

Uses Today

The gift of encouraging is the ability to urge others to grow spiritually. It is the ability to minister to those who are hurting, using words of comfort, encouragement, and counsel. Some ways the gift of encouraging can be used today are:

Personal counseling (on staff or private)
Pastoring
Visiting shut-ins, hospitals, absentees
Helping in funeral follow-up
Working with the retarded, handicapped, addicted
Writing notes of encouragement (to missionaries, to anyone)
Serving as a greeter in the church foyer
Assisting a Sunday school teacher
Praying with and for others (intercession)

Exploring the Possibilities

Begin with very simple yet practical things. The next time someone responds "Fine" to your question, "How are you?" stop and find out what's *really* happening in his life. If you learn he is hurting, follow up with a private session between the two of you. Go out to lunch or coffee together and ask some gently probing questions. Listen carefully when he answers you. Let him know you honestly care.

Listen to your answers as well. Are you giving personal opinion or do you automatically counsel with scriptural advice?

Look for ways you can show encouragement to the people around you. If it has been some time since you told your pastor and his wife that you are praying for them, remind them again this week. And then spend a generous portion of time interceding on their behalf.

Get involved in a prayer chain. When a request is passed on to you, follow up with some type of comfort or encouragement to the person involved.

Visit hospitals, nursing homes, retirement centers, and handicapped programs. You may find a special niche in one of those areas.

And don't forget, children and husbands need comfort and encouragement, too.

But what do you do if you are already involved in an area where the ministry of encouragement is needed, and you realize it isn't your gift?

Find someone who has the gift and ask for some pointers. You can learn enough general encouragement skills to help in your current situation.

If you are presently counseling someone, and you know this isn't your best area of service, deliberately look up some scriptures that fit your counselee's problem and pass them on in your next session.

If you need to visit someone in a hospital or nursing home, try to find something positive to say. Since elderly people love to talk about their childhood, search out something positive that will jog their memory, and let them do the talking. For those who are very ill, a simple smile and "I'm praying for you" will do nicely. Stay only a short time. Don't make them feel as if you're hanging around, waiting for them to die.

Most of all, listen to your own words. Avoid as much

negativism as possible. All of us can learn to say things in a more positive way. We all can find something good to say about another person. Tell the church secretary she's doing a good job. Let the custodian know you appreciate what he is doing. Smile—a lot!

Promises to Claim

"But encourage one another daily, as long as it is called Today, so that none of you may be hardened by sin's deceitfulness. We have come to share in Christ if we hold firmly till the end the confidence we had at first" (Heb. 3:13–14).

For Further Study

Luke 3:18; Acts 2:40; 11:23; 14:21–22; 15:32; 20:2; 2 Cor. 9:5; 1 Thess. 2:11–12; 4:1; 5:14; 2 Thess. 3:12; 1 Tim. 2:1, 6:2; 2 Tim. 4:2; Titus 1:9; 2:6, 9, 15; Heb. 10:25; 1 Pet. 5:1, 5:12.

Questions to Ponder

1. Who, among your acquaintances, do you think displays the attributes of an encourager? List them here.

_____

2. To whom could you send a card or note of encouragement today? Do it.
3. In what way have you challenged someone to grow spiritually this past week?
4. Are you the type of person other people automatically turn to for advice when they have a problem? Name some people who have recently (in the past three weeks) said to you, "I just needed someone to talk to" (or words to that effect).

BLESSED ARE THE MERCIFUL

CHAPTER SIX

An hour before dawn Sarah parked her car in front of Howard's home. She knew this elderly saint had few breaths of earthly air left before he would inhale the life-giving atmosphere of heaven. Hurrying up the shadowed walk to the porch, she tapped lightly on the door and entered the dark house.

A night light outlined Howard's bed and enabled Sarah to find a chair. Gratefully, Howard's son smiled at her. "He's about the same," the son whispered. "I'm going to work now. Call me if there's any change." Weariness edged his words, and Sarah knew he had been up most of the night beside his father's bed.

In the silence that ensued, Sarah prayed for Howard, his wife, and his family. She prayed and waited for morning, all the while listening to Howard's rattling gasps.

When bright sunlight bathed the yard, Howard's wife took her turn at the bedside. And, once again Sarah left the quiet neighborhood to go home and fix her husband's breakfast. A few hours later the phone rang and Howard's wife told Sarah he'd gone to be with Jesus.

This wasn't the first time Sarah had helped a family through those painful days and hours of losing someone in death. Only a year earlier she had reached out in love to a family whose teenage daughter was struck and killed by a bus.

"That was really hard for me," she admits. "It brought back so many sad memories of our own son's sudden death in a traffic accident. But these are hurting people and they need someone who understands, someone who will help."

Acts of mercy are often done in quiet ways. Without fanfare or glory, they are given from the hearts of those who care. Privately, compassion flows in unobtrusive ways to heal the hurts of people. Sometimes, the smallest thing eases a moment of hurt.

Biblical Definition

"If it is showing mercy, let him do it cheerfully" (Rom. 12:8).

Another word for mercy is compassion. Wherever this word *mercy* (in Greek, *eleeo*) is written in Scripture, it is used in the verb form. There is action involved. A person is either giving mercy or receiving it. Mercy isn't a treasure to place on a shelf. It's a working gift.

Mercy is something that is *done*. You can speak words of mercy or show mercy through acts of kindness, but it's all done through the power of divine grace.

This word means to feel the suffering of others and to act in a sympathetic way toward them.

Mercy should be rich and full, pouring over another's wounds with deeply penetrating balm. Our world needs mercy, our hometowns need mercy, our families need mercy, and I need mercy. Jesus knew all of this when He planned the cooperation of the members of His body.

Biblical Examples

A man named Onesiphorus was a merciful person. He visited Paul in prison, and Paul says of him, "May the Lord show mercy to the household of Onesiphorus, because he often refreshed me and was not ashamed of my chains. On the contrary, when he was in Rome, he searched hard for me until he found me" (2 Tim. 1:16–17). Onesiphorus didn't just pass by the jail one day and decide to drop in. He had to search to find Paul. It was a deliberate act on his part. Mercy isn't something that just happens. Mercy is a choice, something we do.

Jesus did more recorded acts of mercy than anything else. If you want to know what true mercy is, study the life of Christ.

One day Jesus was walking down the road away from Jericho and two blind men were sitting beside the road. They called out, "Lord, Son of David, have mercy on us." Jesus, in compassion, touched their eyes and immediately their sight was restored. (See Matt. 20:29–34.)

But the prime example is the mercy God has shown to us through salvation. God knew the pain in our lives brought on by sin, and in His greatest act of mercy, He provided healing through the substitutionary death of His Son, Jesus Christ. Only God can show compassion of that magnitude.

We didn't know what we needed. We only felt the pain. He brought healing at the ultimate cost to himself, the very life of His Son.

There are times when we only feel the pain. We may think that alleviation of the pain is the solution and ask specifically for it. But God's best for us may be something entirely different.

Peter and John encountered that type of situation one day as they walked to the temple. Everyone in the area knew about the lame man who sat, begging for alms, beside the gate named Beautiful. The man couldn't work and earn a living, so he asked for money; that was *his* solution. But Peter and John knew of something far better than money.

> Peter looked straight at him, as did John. Then Peter said, "Look at us!" So the man gave them his attention, expecting to get something from them.

> Then Peter said, "Silver or gold I do not have, but what I have I give you. In the name of Jesus Christ of Nazareth, walk." Taking him by the right hand, he helped him up, and instantly the man's feet and ankles became strong. He jumped to his feet and began to walk (Acts 3:4–8).

They gave the man *not* what he asked for but the real solution to ease his suffering. That's mercy!

Compassion in Action

The person with the gift of mercy is one who sees the hurts and does something about them. The pain may be physical, mental, emotional, spiritual, or social. Regardless of the type, the mercy-gifted person will see it and show compassion in some form.

Teri observed a Christian woman (Marla) who was broken and bruised by a divorce, and she had to do something about it. Teri became Marla's friend. When emotions overcame Marla, Teri lovingly placed her arms around the woman and let her cry, crying with her. When it seemed others were socially rejecting Marla, Teri made sure the woman was included. She sat with Marla in church, went shopping with her, baby-sat when needed. Teri listened and loved until time brought its own healing. I'm sure that Marla is more secure today than she would have been without the benefit of Teri's compassion.

Mercy is far more than a reaction to a situation. The mercy-gifted person wants to go beyond acknowledging the pain and actually do something. The woman of mercy *lives* the problem with the other person. She can listen with empathy and comprehend life through the hurting person's eyes.

There are many individuals whom most people overlook. With "God's sense" rather than a sixth sense, the merciful person spots them instantly in a crowd. The woman gifted with mercy can walk through a crowded room and be magnetically drawn to an elderly person sitting alone in a corner. She will take the arm of a person who is new to a group and immediately get to know her, drawing her into the circle of fellowship.

The hungry, the mentally handicapped, the child who needs more attention, the deaf, the blind—all catch the heart of the woman to whom God has granted an abundance of mercy.

Barbara knows the joy of helping one of God's special people. As a teacher, she often gives the extra time and attention a student needs. But one student needed her more than the others.

Brain-damaged by a tragic accident, this student was determined to relearn her lost skills. Day after day she would come to class and struggle through math problems that should have been easy for a girl her age. Again and again, Barbara would explain the principles involved.

"She's one of God's special people, and it's a joy to help her," Barbara explains, shaking off any praise she might receive for the extra work. "When she tries so hard, I have to help her. It's worth it when she learns a concept and can remember it."

Barbara has learned the skills necessary to become a schoolteacher, but one of the prettiest flowers in her spiritual gifts bouquet is mercy.

Are you a woman of mercy? Look at the joys and cautions below. Do they describe you or someone you know?

Characteristic Joys

1. She is sensitive to the emotional needs of others.
2. She is naturally drawn to those in distress.
3. She has a deep desire to ease pain and to bring healing.
4. Prayer is a very important part of her life.
5. She easily discerns sincere motives on the part of others.
6. She can view things from the other person's point of view and is an empathetic listener.
7. She receives a blessing from visiting nursing homes, hospitals, jails, or the homes of shut-ins.
8. She receives a special joy from working with people who are ignored by others.
9. Tears spring to her eyes easily.
10. She enjoys being around other people.

Characteristic Cautions

1. She is usually guided by her emotions rather than logic and can be easily hurt. She is subject to depression and a martyr complex.
2. She can easily become too familiar and inquisitive.
3. She seems to lack the ability to be firm and can't make decisions under stress.

4. Others may view her as weak and indecisive because she can't stand to hurt anyone in a confrontation of words or actions.

Edna is a mercy person and, typically, she has trouble confronting others when they need it. Edna runs a restaurant and has several employees. If there is a problem among the staff, Edna tries to smooth things over by being kind to each person in hopes that the problem will go away. "I don't want to hurt them," she explains. "They know they ought to work according to the rules. If I give them enough time, they'll change."

But in some cases that doesn't work. There are times when she needs to tell an employee, "Either do the work or you'll be fired." That's difficult for her to do. She needs encouragement from a more assertive personality to confront her staff when necessary.

People who are gifted with mercy don't appreciate people who "bark a lot of orders." Gentleness is the key. Mercy people react poorly to stress and harshness. If they are confronted by a pressure situation, they will not be able to make decisions.

If You Score Low in Mercy

If you are low in mercy, don't consistently work with the elderly or very young children. These people are very sensitive and although you don't mean to hurt them, your level of insensitivity may cause them pain. Does this mean never work with them? Of course not.

After I took a spiritual gifts evaluation and discovered that my mercy level was extremely low, I asked God to help me in this area. Very soon He brought an elderly gentleman into my life. Quiet, sensitive, and needing a friend, he became God's instrument in raising my mercy level.

His children are missionaries, and "Grandpa," as I call him, needed a surrogate daughter. In place of his son, I handle the intricate details of caring for an elderly parent. Together, he and I recently selected a new retirement home for him. When he needed to go to the hospital, he called me. When insurance papers were confusing, he asked me for an explanation. More importantly, when he needs an ice cream cone or a walk in the park . . . you guessed it.

This relationship has done so much for me that I'd hate to give it up, even if Grandpa's family should come back. I've learned to listen, really listen to the hurts and sageness of a vintage saint. It isn't natural for me to slow down and take time to be that sensitive. But God is helping me learn how. I'm acquiring a new skill.

Being low in mercy has other drawbacks. Counseling may be unsuccessful because you won't easily discern the hurts or emotions of the counselee. Those who are ill may make you uncomfortable or even irritated. In this case, you might consider *not* being a nurse!

How can you demonstrate mercy to others when this isn't your best gift? One of the things you can do is watch your words. Do you answer others too quickly. Choose carefully how you reply. Use a softer tone, and select gentle words.

Another thing you can do is ask God to help you with your attitude. Every person in the world carries some type of hurt, from the tiniest child to the one with a wrinkled face. As you walk through your day, try with God's help to become more attuned to the needs around you. Pray, "Lord, help me with my attitude in this situation. Help me to see these people through your eyes, to treat them with your love." We will grow spiritually when we stretch ourselves to emulate the mercy of Christ.

If You Score High in Mercy

If you are a mercy person, remember that you react emotionally to others around you. You can easily get so involved in others' lives that you neglect your own. If you get too wrapped up in the other person's hurt, taking it on as your own, this can harm the person rather than helping her overcome the problem.

Some people tend to take advantage of the merciful person. But if you have that gift, you probably won't see what they're doing. Find someone who is *not* a mercy person, who will help you evaluate what's happening in your life. Listen to her if she tells you someone is taking advantage of you.

People do need help, but you can go too far and do too much. You need to know when to quit, and that's tough for a mercy person to do alone.

The person you are helping may only have a temporary hurt. She will get over it. But you, as a mercy person, can get so wrapped up in the problem that you will continue to feel the emotion of the situation. Learn where the limits are and follow them.

Young single girls especially need to know their limitations. Although prison ministries are especially important to those gifted with mercy, young girls should avoid visitation in prisons or jails. They may become too involved with those who are in distress.

I worked for a time in our county juvenile court system and saw, from the inside, some devastating situations. The prisoners actually discuss ways to get people's sympathy and to take advantage of "those suckers on the outside!"

There are hurting people behind bars who need our compassion and assistance. But young single girls are too vulnerable. They need protection, too.

Most mercy-gifted people need to avoid stressful situations that require immediate decisions. They need calm, quiet times to make careful choices.

You may find it difficult to work with the person who is insensitive to the hurts of others, or argumentative, opinionated, and forceful.

In counseling you may not be strong enough to confront the counselee with the truth or be firm enough to insist that they follow God's laws.

Varying Approaches

One particular year in my life was so trying that I wasn't sure I'd survive it. Because the problems were personal, I didn't feel I could tell others what I was going through, yet the pain was intense.

One day Carol saw my pain and lovingly invited me to her home for a cup of tea. I'm not sure exactly what she saw, but her concern was genuine. Compassion is concern plus love, and that's what Carol showed me. Three cups of tea later (brewed the way they do it in England, slow and precise, rich and aromatic), I had told her everything I was going through.

I didn't know she had experienced a similar situation, but her face said, "Tell me all!" She didn't give me any advice. She just listened and helped me through that trying time. Still today, Carol supports me with her love and compassion. Taped to the wall beside my desk is a card Carol sent several years ago. It says in part, "I care about what happens to you. . . . I'm here to talk whenever you need me." She's now a missionary in Indonesia where she brings her God-given gift of compassion to forgotten people, hidden people, hurting people who need to experience God's love in action.

All Christians are expected to show mercy to each other and to strangers. But those gifted with mercy see the suffering world and have an inner need to reach out with help, comfort, healing, and joy. They want to make the situation better. The mercy person not only sees the suffering around the world, she is able to communicate those needs to others who can do something about it.

Lela knew how to do that. A Sunday school child showed up in church barefoot one day. It was summer and I supposed the child had forgotten or didn't want to wear shoes. I didn't think any more about it, but Lela reacted.

On Tuesday Lela visited that child in his home and learned that the parents were out of work and out of money. Illness had taken what little they had. Lela contacted another woman who was able to buy the shoes and supply some of the other family needs.

That's an example of the body of Christ functioning as it should. Mercy sees the need and makes it known to others who can provide the solution.

It was mercy that caused the world to know about the starvation in Ethiopia. We would never have heard about the famine, except perhaps in statistics, had not people with mercy been moved to do something. The outpouring of compassion that resulted shows that the world community can act in a merciful way. Mercy saw the need, Administration organized an avenue of response, and Giving supplied the aid.

The body of Christ needs to function in the same way. Sometimes we cloister ourselves within our church walls and forget about the suffering world. We forget that for some inner-city families in America, suffering and starvation are a way of life. Here is a whole area of service crying out for mercy people to become involved and to involve others.

The body of Christ needs those gifted with mercy. Mercy people make us aware of the hurts of others (whether physical, emotional, or spiritual). Mercy initiates reconciliation and breaks down barriers.

Uses Today

The ministry of mercy is the ability to empathize with the hurting and to cheerfully, compassionately act to relieve the suffering.

Cheerfully! If you are gifted in mercy, those gentle acts you do will spread its glow all through you. Your smile and even laughter when the hurting is great may bring immeasurable joy to others. Many of us do merciful acts, but some of us *don't* do them cheerfully!

How does this gift of mercy fit into the body of Christ? Who needs it for what types of ministries? Some suggestions are listed below. See if you can add others.

> Serving in any "compassionate ministries"
> Teaching Sunday school
> Visiting shut-ins, hospitals, jails, prisons
> Visiting anyone in need
> Identifying and reporting to others when someone is in distress
> Participating in a prayer chain
> Working in the church nursery
> Helping with handicapped ministries
> Foster parenting
> Participating in a hospice program
> Working as a doctor or nurse

Exploring the Possibilities

Take a moment to evaluate yourself. Have we described you, even somewhat, in this chapter? Do you think you are the type of person who can help the hurting? Try volunteering at your local hospital for a month. Work in your church nursery or visit people in a nursing home one day each week.

Look at the categories we listed above. Select one and get involved in that activity in some way.

After a month, reevaluate. How did you feel about what you were doing?

Promise to Claim

"Blessed are the merciful, for they will be shown mercy" (Matt. 5:7).

For Further Study

Matt. 9:27; 15:22–28; 18:21–35; 25:34–40; Rom. 9:15–16; 2 Cor. 4:1; Phil. 2:27; 1 Tim. 1:12–16; Jude 21–23; 1 Pet. 2:10.

Questions to Ponder

1. Name someone you know who is hurting in some way. What can you do to ease that hurt today?
2. What is your favorite way of showing love, care, and compassion to others?
3. How have you shown mercy to someone this week?
4. What area of personal hurt do you need to tell someone about so the situation can be alleviated?

GIVING WITH JOY

CHAPTER SEVEN

The sun glinted off the trash can in the school yard, catching Alice's attention. "There's a big one," she said, pointing ahead. "Let's see if there are any pop cans inside."

She and her friend Mary, both past 60, were on their usual morning walk. In minutes they were head down, rummaging through the rubbish, pulling out pop cans, beer bottles, and anything else that could be recycled.

Suddenly Mary raised up and laughed. "Alice, what would people think if they saw us? Two old ladies digging through the garbage must be quite a sight!"

"You're right," Alice said, depositing a large bottle in her sack. "But it's for the Lord's work, so I don't care what they think."

Alice and Mary are just two of a group of people in their town who recycle bottles, cans, and papers to raise funds for missions. Retired and on fixed incomes, they find it difficult to come up with extra money for supporting missionaries. But recycling has become for them a gleanable field, ripe for harvest.

Yet Alice and Mary and the rest of the people in their group don't merely send in their donations. They all regularly correspond with the missionaries they support. Once a month they meet to share news from each of their missionaries and pray for them. Some from their group have traveled to the mission field to see for themselves what is happening. And when the missionaries are on furlough, these supporters visit with them, give them lodging in their homes, and do whatever they can to help.

This is hands-on giving. Working with their hands to bring in the funds needed, they keep a firm interest in the projects to which they give. Alice and Mary and the rest of their group demonstrate exactly what Paul has written in Romans about the spiritual gift of giving.

Biblical Definition

"If it is contributing to the needs of others, let him give generously" (Rom. 12:8). One translation says to give with simplicity, and another uses the word *liberality*. The word can also mean *bountifulness*.

Notice that even the translators have difficulty agreeing on what word to use to convey the original meaning for the ministry of giving.

The Greek word for giving or contributing is *metadidomi*. It means "to give," but it also includes a sharing in the giving. This word comes from two other words. The first part, *meta*, means "participation" in the transfer of the gift from one to the other. *Didomi*, the second part, is the basic "to give" verb.

There is more to this word than the idea of giving. Suppose I gave you a piece of paper with some scriptures to read (like the ones you find at the end of each of these chapters) and walk away. Giving you the piece of paper is the *didomi* part of this word. But if I say, "Let's go over these scriptures together tomorrow and discuss them," that's the *meta* part of the word. Not only is the giver a personal participant in the giving, but there is a lingering involvement in the transfer of the gift.

In the five places I found this word in the New Testament, only the Rom. 12:8 passage translates it as *give*.

In Rom. 1:11–12, where Paul is talking about spiritual gifts, the word is translated *impart*. "I long to see you that I may *impart* to you some spiritual gift to make you strong—that is, that you and I may be mutually encouraged by each other's faith."

In 1 Thess. 2:8 it's translated *share*. Paul is talking about sharing the gospel as well as their lives with the new believers. He doesn't say to just give their testimony and walk away. He urges the Thessalonians to share the gospel with the new believers and stay involved.

Luke 3:11 uses this word also in the sense of sharing. John the Baptist was trying to show his hearers a new lifestyle. "The man with two tunics should *share* with him who has none, and the one who has food should do the same." It doesn't mean to hand over your coat and let him walk away with it, never seeing him again. It means to *give what is needed and stay involved.*

Eph. 4:28 also uses the word *share*. "He . . . must work, doing something useful with his own hands, that he may have something to share [*metadidomi*] with those in need."

So, when Rom. 12:8 talks about the ministry of giving, it means more than a business deduction on the IRS form. There is personal involvement in the act of giving as well as the imparting of the gift itself.

This type of giving doesn't come out of a sense of duty

or because of high-pressure techniques. It is generated from deep within the giver. There is a God-woven thread inside people with the gift of giving that causes them to respond personally and liberally when a specific need is observed.

Those who minister by giving don't stop with the common tithe. More than fulfilling a responsibility, they give abundantly out of the bounty God has given to them. Yet givers are very discerning; they know when to give and when to withhold.

Biblical Examples

Paul uses a marvelous example of *metadidomi*, the spiritual type of giving, in 2 Cor. 8:1–15. The Macedonians were in the midst of severe trials, yet they begged for the privilege of sharing in Paul's ministry.

Notice that the Macedonians were not responding to a request from Paul for money, but rather there was a self-generated urgency from the people themselves to give. They saw his need and the needs of the ministry and responded.

In today's society we tend to get the giving process backwards. Someone stands before us, on TV or in a sanctuary, and gives an appeal. The closer the appeal is to Hollywood's production standards, the more people give. Unfortunately, a lot of people respond to this kind of hype. But, the gift is not supposed to be solicited by the person or ministry in need. According to the intent of Scripture, the giver is the one who initiates the transfer process in response to God's prompting.

If we follow the biblical principle, this also does away with heavy pressure requests for money. Have you ever been in a service where someone stood in front and said, "I need 14 people who will give $100 (or $1000) and 25 people who will give $50"? The amount of money requested doesn't matter. The point is, the ones gifted with giving will respond quietly to legitimate needs. They don't require a huckster approach. When this type of pressure occurs, somebody isn't following biblical principles!

God-gifted givers usually prefer that their gifts be anonymous, if possible. At least they will want it handled discreetly. Public display would either embarrass them or turn them off from the project completely.

Yes, we need to be informed of needs, but the one with the ministry of giving seems to have access to God's eyes to perceive those special needs without a lot of hype. They have eyes, just like the mercy-gifted person, but givers have *hands* and *resources* to go with the eyes.

Characteristic Joys

As we look at the characteristic joys of the ministry of giving, remember that the first four do not refer to *financial* giving only. Someone could *need* encouragement, for example. Notice the blending of gifts. The person whose bouquet has large Mercy blossoms or Encouraging flowers is going to be sensitive to needs, too.

1. She has the ability to detect unnoticed needs.

2. She prefers to meet needs quietly without any publicity.

3. She tends to involve and motivate others in her giving projects.

4. She gets personally involved in whatever ministry is being supported.

5. She tends to make wise purchases.

6. She likes to give gifts which have long-range value.

7. She is a good money manager and can't stand to be in debt (in any area—not just financial, but social, too).

8. She seems to be able to acquire money or resources constantly.

9. She receives great pleasure from giving to God's work.

10. She doesn't give reluctantly or out of a sense of duty, but responds to any need cheerfully.

Characteristic Cautions

1. She is very thrifty, personally, and some people may see that as being selfish.

2. By her giving she tends to control other people and projects.

3. When she resists *pressure* to give, others may see that as a lack of generosity.

4. Because she is materially or money-oriented, she gives the appearance of having a worldly value system.

Varying Approaches

Giving can be material and spiritual. Typical material aid would be things like clothes, shelter, food, and money. The spiritual type of giving includes imparting faith and encouragement, as well as sharing our lives.

Marilyn Lazlo has chosen to spend her life sharing the gospel with a tribe of Indonesian people who are virtually hidden from the rest of the world. She lives in a hut like they do, she wears simple clothes, and of course doesn't drive a car. Her lifestyle is way below what it would have been if she had remained in the United States. Her work with this tribe of people was documented in a film entitled *Mountain of Light.*

A man in the Southwest saw this film and contacted Wycliffe Bible Translators, the organization with which Marilyn is affiliated. "I want to give Marilyn one of my oil wells," he said. (This was back when oil wells were worth lots of money.) Of course the gift went to support missions, not her personally, but notice he was giving *one of his oil wells*, out of his abundance.

Here we have the two kinds of giving, material and spiritual. Both Marilyn and the man were giving out of the abundance of what God gave them. The outward signs look so different, yet they are part of the same gift. And, they are equal in God's sight.

The person with the spiritual gift of giving, then, will probably find herself in one or both of these two categories:

1. *When God allows continuous excess flow of money and goods.*

It's easy for this person to make money. She doesn't have to be a Wall Street genius. In fact, the plain hard laborer fits well into this category. Financial success seems to be drawn to her magnetically.

Have you ever known somebody who could walk down a street and have more money in her pocket at the end of the block than when she started? Most of us end up with our pockets empty, and we're not sure how it happened. But for the one God has gifted with *metadidomi*, especially in the material form, the flow of money and materials is easy.

Gloria is an antique collector. Her greatest delight is finding a bargain at a yard sale, scraping off the dirt, and revealing a priceless treasure. Starting out in the morning, driving down the street, she may stop at several house sales to sift through the jumble of castoffs. A few hours later she cleans up the treasures she's unearthed and sorts them according to the people she knows will buy them.

From one collector to another, one dealer to another, she plies her trade. What cost her nickles and dimes will easily become dollars. By the end of the day Gloria makes a satisfactory deposit in the bank and returns home.

But Gloria's work doesn't stop there. She helps support missionaries as well as her local church's "Cup of Cold Water" program. Both of these projects will receive a hefty chunk of her profits.

I can go with Gloria to those same places and not find a thing worthwhile. The only explanation I have is that God has gifted Gloria with His eyes. Those are His bargains, and Gloria becomes His hands and feet.

Norma, an executive in a large firm, is another person who seems to be magnetic when it comes to finances. In God's unique way, He brings project after project to Norma's attention, and each one is equally successful. She doesn't seem to do anything different than anyone else. Her work is hard and exacting and Norma gives it her full energy. But success just happens.

Yet, the financial reward for her hard work is what she gives back to God. Norma's giving is quiet and methodical. The practical things are her focus for giving. She is heavily involved in her local church, funding whatever project is current. Whether it's a new bus, carpet replacement, or roof repairs, Norma contributes from the abundance God has given to her.

2. *When God makes it easy to give.*

This giver may not be overwhelmingly wealthy, but she simply doesn't need all that God gives her. It doesn't bother her at all to live in substandard housing. That may be her choice. She doesn't seem to need as much money and goods to get along in this world. It certainly doesn't mean she is lazy. In fact, she is usually a hard worker.

When I was growing up, my closest girlfriend, Lillian, and I often talked about becoming missionaries. Lillian never lost sight of her goal. After she finished college, she added training as a Licensed Practical Nurse and moved to Mexico. In a short time she met and married a man from

England who was also a missionary, and together they focused their attention on the hidden tribes of Brazil.

With their education, both Lillian and her husband could have lived quite comfortably in either England or the United States. Instead, using the gifts God has given them, they chose to give—everything. Lillian's letters tell about drifting down the flooded Amazon in a boat with a motor that conked out, about miscarrying a baby in the jungle, about baking biscuits on a stove made from mud and a coffee can.

But she also writes about teaching the Indians how to bathe their babies, how to plant and grow crops, and most importantly, how to pray. Together she and her husband are using all their talents and training to bring the gospel to these people who would never hear about God in any other way.

I'm afraid most of us would focus on the cost. We'd consider her lifestyle a heavy deprivation. But God has gifted Lillian with the ability to give her life in this way.

What do you do if you have a giving heart but not money? Give out of the abundance that God gives to you. Whatever gift He has given to you, that's the abundance to give from. Has He given you the gift of serving? Then serve abundantly. Has He given you the gift of teaching? Then teach abundantly. Not everything is measured in dollars. There is spiritual sharing, faith sharing, encouragement sharing. All are part of the gift or ministry of giving.

In 2 Cor. 8:12 it says, "For if the willingness is there, the gift is acceptable according to what one has, not according to what he does not have." Underline this in your Bible!

I know people who think they *have* to give every time a request is made, whether or not they can honestly get along without that money.

Karen regularly tithes, sometimes double tithes, and is quick to write a check whenever an appeal is made. The problem is, Karen and her family have very little income. They are regularly scraping the bottom of the barrel to buy groceries or pay their bills.

Karen's Christian testimony suffers each time businessmen have to return her bounced checks or wait months to be paid for their work and goods.

The person who has a giving heart but not the spiritual gift of giving may be giving sacrificially because she sees the great need, but her giving hurts her family circumstances. This person is the one who can't quite make ends meet but puts a larger check in the offering plate than most people do. She has difficulty paying her bills yet overpays financially when it comes to God's work. If this person gave a more appropriate amount—let's say the ten percent noted in Scripture—her personal needs would be met.

God knows to whom He can trust an abundance of money and goods. He gives those people the spiritual ministry of giving. Remember, that word *gifts* means *grace*. If the giving can be done graciously, out of God's abundance, then it's right.

If You Score Low in Giving

If you don't have this gift, remember that it is God whom you serve. He knows your individual circumstances. Avoid high-pressure appeals for money, especially if you are a mercy-gifted person. Take plenty of time before you sign a pledge card and pray until you know exactly what God requires of you.

If I could etch this next statement in gold, I would. Remember, there is no glory for God if you give generously and the check bounces at the bank or you can't pay your bills the next month. If we can't pay our bills, where is

God's glory? Christians in great debt tarnish God's glory.

Many business people have told me, "I don't want to do business with Christians. They don't pay their bills."

If giving is low among your spiritual gifts, does that mean you don't have to give? What do you do when there are needs but you don't have the resources to meet them?

Look to see which of your resources is renewable. If God has given you the ministry of giving, then He will consistently renew your resources. If your renewable resource isn't monetary, then perhaps your giving could be the sharing of the gospel or the sharing of your life with others.

Be discerning in your giving. The pumpkin farmer may eat some of his own crop, but he'll save the seeds to plant next year. Do your best to create a renewable resource.

Check your motives and feelings when you give. Are you giving so that others will know that you gave? Be honest. Is there an inner reluctance to part with that money? To the one with the ministry of giving, there is deep pleasure and great joy in contributing.

If You Score High in Giving

Remember that you have a tendency to control other people because you have the resources to meet their needs. Allow God to work through you, but don't try to manipulate the object of your giving. It's God's gift; you are only the instrument through which He gives to others.

Also, be careful that your trait of thriftiness doesn't hurt others around you. Are you scrimping too much in one area in order to give in another? For example, a wife may be gifted as a giver, but she may be so tightfisted with the family income that she doesn't give her own children the material things they need.

Taking shoes away from your own children to give them to a poor child isn't what God planned. Feeding your husband mashed potato sandwiches in order to send a gift to the missionaries doesn't properly meet the need.

Don't forget that the gift has no value if it's given without love. "If I give all I possess to the poor and surrender my body to the flames, but have not love, I gain nothing" (1 Cor. 13:3).

The true giver prefers not to be known as the source of the gift. Her satisfaction comes in knowing that a need has been met. If a mistake were made and her gift were attributed to someone else, she'd probably never tell anyone or correct it. The gift is more important to her than receiving the credit.

The ministry of giving is the unique ability God gives to certain people to share spiritual and material resources generously and cheerfully to enhance the work of the Lord.

If the giving glorifies God, then the gift enhances the work of the Lord. Be discriminating in your giving. Ask yourself, "Does this gift really glorify God?" Spiritual gifts are given for the purpose of building up the body of Christ.

There are people and organizations that will take as much of your money, time, and energies as they can. Maybe you have a deadbeat brother-in-law who is a mooch. He won't work and wants you to support him. Where is the glory for God in this? Scripture says we are to work with our own hands (Eph. 4:28). It also says if we don't work, we shouldn't be allowed to eat (2 Thess. 3:10). Does it glorify God to perpetuate your brother-in-law's lazy behavior? Make sure your gift glorifies God.

If we function in our giving as a group, greater needs can be met. The Apostle Paul's Christian friends couldn't all afford to go on a missionary journey, but collectively they made it possible for him to go.

Uses Today

Why did God feel this gift is necessary to the body of Christ? Perhaps of all the gifts, this one is the easiest to place. Very simply, it takes money and resources to keep churches and ministries functioning. But churches and ministries aren't the only focus we are to have. From time to time there are specific individual needs that need to be met also.

How can this gift be used today in the body of Christ? Listed below are some suggested areas of giving. There are others, of course, and you could write some of your own suggestions here, too.

Paying the bills: Focus on the local body and help pay the bills that keep the church operating (building maintenance and repair, utility bills, Sunday school supplies).

Spreading the gospel: Pastors and staff need salaries. Missions, missionaries, and related ministries need financial support (e.g., home mission churches, prison ministries, homes for unwed mothers and street people).

Meeting specific individual needs: The child with no shoes, the family out of work that needs groceries, the person overwhelmed by medical bills.

Funding projects: Building funds, other extra projects that don't come under the heading of monthly bills.

Exploring the Possibilities

What about this ministry of giving? How can you explore it on your own?

Begin on your knees with an open Bible in front of you. No giving should be initiated without God's specific guidance. If you are a mature Christian, then follow exactly what God gives you to do.

If you are a new Christian, test the waters slowly. As

God lays a specific project on your heart, get involved carefully. Watch to see how God guides and how He renews the source of your giving. If it's money He's asking you to give, give of the fruit . . . not the root. That plant needs to grow and supply more fruit. If it's time, energy, etc., give from the abundance.

Look at the above list. Is there a burden on your heart for one of those areas? Ask your pastor for guidance in becoming involved.

Promises to Claim

"Each man should give what he has decided in his heart to give, not reluctantly or under compulsion, for God loves a cheerful giver" (2 Cor. 9:7).

" 'Bring the whole tithe into the storehouse, that there may be food in my house. Test me in this,' says the Lord Almighty, 'and see if I will not throw open the floodgates of heaven and pour out so much blessing that you will not have room enough for it' " (Mal. 3:10).

For Further Study

Deut. 16:17; Ezra 2:69; Neh. 13:10; Matt. 6:1–4; Mark 12:41–44; Luke 12:48b; Acts 3:1–6; 4:36–37; 11:29; 1 Cor. 16:2.

Questions to Ponder

1. What specifically is your renewable resource?
2. How can you become involved in meeting the needs of others, whether it's financial or spiritual?
3. Is your giving done out of obligation or is it done cheer-

fully? (*Cheerfully* means *hilariously*. Does your giving add such zing that you want to bubble with laughter?)

4. What specific needs or burdens is God placing on your heart?

SERVING WITH LOVE

CHAPTER EIGHT

Snow clogged Shirley's boots as she unlocked the door to the church kitchen. This was the third day—third *long* day—she had spent preparing for tonight's dinner. She pulled off her boots and placed them neatly beside the back door and switched on the lights. December mornings were dark at this hour.

"Oh, good," she said aloud. "The tables are all in place." Her voice echoed in the empty multipurpose room. She plugged in the coffeepot and stuffed the large pans of salads she had brought from home into the over-sized refrigerators.

All day she worked quietly and efficiently, baking rolls, stirring simmering pots, and arranging table decorations. By evening the room smelled like Christmas and glowed with red candles nestled in fresh pine boughs.

Church dinners were Shirley's special place of service. Tonight's dinner would bring her church family together for the purpose of showering love gifts on the pastor and family of a small neighboring church.

Late in the afternoon her husband arrived in a van loaded with her personal silver trays and bowls plus several gallons of punch she had made the evening before. A few minutes later the other members of the food committee entered the kitchen, bearing plates of delightful desserts.

By the time the church members bustled in, cheeks rosy from the crisp weather, Shirley had wrapped herself in a new Christmas apron. She listened as the pianist tested the ivory keys and drifted into "O Come, All Ye Faithful." In a nearby corner, scores of carefully selected gifts and boxes of food piled in front of a sparkling Christmas tree with handmade decorations.

Shirley surveyed the room, now full of laughing, happy people who had come to share their bounty with others. She smiled. This was a labor of love.

Serving is Shirley's gift; serving *in love* is her style. She shows her love for the Lord best through doing His quiet work.

Biblical Definition

"If it is serving, let him serve" (Rom. 12:7).

The Greek word *diakonia* is used to describe this gift of serving. It comes from the word *diako*, which means "to run on errands."

We understand it to mean serving or attending (to others), aiding, ministering, giving relief. It includes the idea of waiting on tables or doing other menial duties. Variations of this word also refer to a Christian teacher, pastor, deacon, or deaconess.

Biblical Examples

In fact, this is where the word *deacon* originated. The first deacons weren't black-frocked, top-hatted gents stalking the aisles with Bibles under their arms. Who were the first deacons, and what did they do? Stephen and Philip were among the first seven selected. (See Acts 6:3–6.) Their job? They were *table waiters* who took over the menial tasks, like dividing up the food, so that the apostles could concentrate on their ministries.

"So the Twelve gathered all the disciples together and said, 'It would not be right for us to neglect the ministry of the word of God in order to wait on tables' " (Acts 6:2).

That's exactly what this ministry is: taking care of the menial tasks—whatever they are—in order to free up others so that *their* ministry can go on.

In Bible times, women were thought of as no better than cattle. But fortunately, the Apostle Luke was sensitive to the value of women. He saw their labor, their love, their joys, and their sorrows. And he recorded for us one of the best examples of a woman with the gift of serving.

Luke 10:38–42 introduces us to Martha, who opened up her home to Jesus and His followers. She was so busy with the detailed preparations that she was temporarily distracted from the message of Christ. Yet Martha loved her Lord, too, and she chose to show her love by the labors of her hands.

Serving isn't limited to the kitchen, however. Scripture often refers to the idea of serving one another in every facet of our ministry. The general ministry of preaching and teaching is actually that of serving.

In the Apostle Paul's farewell to the Ephesians, he said, "If only I may . . . complete the task the Lord Jesus has given me—the task of testifying to the gospel of God's grace" (Acts 20:24).

The New Testament gives other examples of those who served the Lord in various ways.

"You know that the household of Stephanas were the first converts in Achaia, and they have devoted themselves to the service of the saints" (1 Cor. 16:15).

And there are plenty of scriptural exhortations to prepare ourselves and use our gifts in service to one another and the Lord.

"It was [Christ] who gave [spiritual gifts] to prepare God's people for works of service, so that the body of Christ may be built up" (Eph. 4:12).

But I think the example I like best is that of Dorcas. Acts 9:36 introduces Dorcas as a woman "who was always doing good and helping the poor." Verse 39 adds the part I like about her sewing. After Dorcas died, "all the widows stood around [Peter], crying and showing him the robes and other clothing that Dorcas had made while she was still with them."

Skill vs. Gift

I guess Dorcas is my favorite example because there was always a sewing machine at our house. As soon as I was big enough to sit on my mother's lap, she began teaching me to sew. Later, my stepmother helped me with tailoring projects. In school I was taught to sew very, very carefully. I learned exactly how to tie the knots and trim the seams. Everything was done "just so."

Once, when we were making skirts at school, another girl in my class whacked the cloth, zipped down a seam, and zap—she was done. She put the skirt on and it looked fine. To get the task done that quickly, she must have known some shortcuts. While I was still stitching and tying, she was done. My sewing skills were carefully learned, but hers seemed to be so natural. While I enjoyed the precision of sewing, I marveled at her ability to breeze through all our projects and move on to something new faster than the rest of us.

Serving Is Practical

There are several ladies in my church who use their gift of serving in the area of sewing. Last year at our missionary convention, we were all surprised by a sanctuary full of flags. These women had sewn a flag, in full color and size, for every country in which our denomination has a missionary. Now, when a missionary comes to speak to us, the flag of the nation where he or she serves stands proudly beside the pulpit.

Countless people have received clothing gifts lovingly made by these ladies. I remember the delightful smile that sparkled on one seamstress's face when she quietly slipped a brand-new blouse into the hands of a visiting pastor's wife from England. Love was stitched into every seam.

Although these ladies may blush when they read this, their hands remain busy serving the Lord they love, just as Dorcas did. They, and others like them, don't want any recognition. They simply want to serve in quiet ways, making life better for others.

Serving is sometimes known as the gift or ministry of helps. The major characteristic of this gift is that it increases the effectiveness of other ministries. While those gifted with mercy often work directly with the needy and hurting, those gifted in serving usually assist other Christians in their ministry.

All of our gifts are serving gifts; they are equal in the building up of the body of Christ. Just because this one is listed as an ''assisting'' ministry doesn't mean it is *less important* than any other.

Those gifted with serving don't try to get by with the least amount of effort possible. On the contrary, they abound in their service to others.

One Sunday after a beautiful communion service, I left the church a bit later than usual, going out through the kitchen door. There, in seclusion, was a group of six or seven ladies, busily washing the communion cups. I was struck by their joyful banter as they washed and dried the cups, replacing them in the trays for the next service.

How often had I sipped from the cup and left it behind with no thought of how many hands it took to wash and dry it? If it were left to me, I'd probably give up after the first drudging session with soap suds!

Serving-gifted people don't differentiate between jobs they *want* to do and those they *like* to do. Rather, they do a task because it's there and needs to be done. The server also seems to abound in energy. When the rest of us have worn out, Serving is still washing cups (cooking, cleaning, pounding nails), wondering where everyone else is!

Most people gifted in serving would rather do the work than sit back and give directions. They would rather spend hours hand-stitching a quilt than write a check to pay for the supplies.

Kari is like that. She is probably one of the busiest ladies I know. She serves on more committees than I can keep track of. And she's always making or baking something. When Kari assists a Sunday-school teacher, she thinks up fun crafts for the kids to do.

For the past two years Kari has served on a committee that plans the ladies' retreat for her church. She brought more ideas for handmade gifts than the rest of the committee put together. When it came time to make them, Kari was a whirlwind, doing far more than her share. She would rather make the gifts than buy them.

The server is generally a cheerful worker. You can always tell the difference between people gifted in serving and those who are just doing a job. The server is the one who smiles and bubbles all the time her hands are busy. There are no frowns and grumbles from her. This is her way of showing love not only for others but for Jesus, too.

There is a higher percentage of serving gifts within the body than any others. If you've read through all these chapters and haven't yet found your gift, this could easily be yours. Serving-gifted people are the *action* people, those who *do* things.

Read through the following list of characteristics and see how many of them describe people you know.

Characteristic Joys

1. She is usually practical in approach, and short-term goals attract her.

2. She is quickly aware of practical needs.

3. She enjoys being involved in hands-on projects.

4. She seems to have an extra measure of physical stamina.

5. She is strongly motivated to complete her tasks.

6. She will gladly inconvenience herself in order to help others.

7. She is always involved in a number of activities.

8. Doing things cheerfully is her way to show love.

9. She is a good worker and willingly does whatever task needs doing.

10. She is a good follower and very flexible.

Characteristic Cautions

1. She will sometimes let people take advantage of her.

2. For her, spiritual things tend to get lost in the focus on practical things.

3. She may be seen as a pushy person.

4. She may resent people who don't want to "serve."

5. She willingly cuts corners in order to complete a task.

As we grow in the Lord, these negatives will diminish. This is a normal part of our spiritual growth. No one is 100% Serving. Neither are they 100% of any of the other gifts. Remember the bouquet? Your other gifts may blend together to help tone down the negative characteristics.

Sandy has an interesting bouquet of serving and administration gifts. Last year she was in charge of the Christmas pageant for her church. In her bustle to get a program together and find people to fill all the parts, she approached Dan. "I'm doing the Christmas program and I want you to be one of the shepherds," she said. "We'll practice the next two Saturdays, and I'll need you to stop by my house on Thursday evening so I can fix your costume."

Sandy wasn't watching Dan's face as she talked. Her attention focused on the list in her hands. When she finally looked up because of the silence, she was surprised to see a frown on his face.

"No," Dan replied simply. And whirling on his heel, he walked away.

Sandy, like other servers, tend to get so caught up in what they are *doing* that they forget other people may not be as enthused about the project. If you have the gift of serving, teach yourself to be aware of the reactions of people around you. Don't just plow somebody down. Be sensitive.

If you are trying to identify people with the gift of serving, look for those who enjoy assisting others no matter what the task. Look for people who spend long hours, great energy, and their own money, if necessary, to finish a project.

Often, there is only one server in a marriage relationship. Either the wife or the husband will be the busy one, while the partner takes a supporting role. But Val and John are both servers.

When they aren't hosting a gaggle of teens in their basement, they're involved in a building project in Peru. Or Val will be in the church nursery hanging new curtains while John is working on the plumbing in the basement. No task is too menial for them, no price too high, no joy so great as meeting a need.

If you want to identify those with the ministry of serving, also look for behind-the-scenes people who aren't too interested in getting credit for what they do, people who only want to meet needs.

Donna is one who doesn't want any credit for her serving. "Everyone can be a server," she says. Very quietly, over a number of years, Donna fixed extra meal portions and carried a tray to her elderly neighbor. If she hadn't brought him a hot meal every day, he would have had to move to a nursing home. But with Donna's help, he lived his last years comfortably in his own home.

Very few people knew she had served in this way, but that's how Donna wants it. She doesn't want any credit for her serving; she only wants to meet needs.

The world and the body of Christ are full of needs. It takes practical people doing practical things to get the job done. Serving is the *grease* that keeps the machinery of Christ's kingdom *moving*.

If God had not given this gift to the body of Christ, many people would get bogged down in their ministries by menial tasks. How many projects would be abandoned for lack of hands, energy, and money?

If You Score Low in Serving

If you don't have this gift, you'll be frustrated by any behind-the-scenes menial tasks. You might want to avoid *constantly* working on kitchen committees, setting up chairs, cleaning up after other people.

Notice the word *constantly*. It's not that you are above doing these things or that you can't or shouldn't do them, but you may find yourself lacking in the joy that ought to pervade this area. You may find you are the irritant factor in an otherwise smoothly operating committee or group.

Avoid situations where others may get credit for what you are doing.

One of my good friends is a writer. She is excellent in her work and has received much acclaim. However, one of her writing projects became a burden to her. Although she worked very hard and produced a wonderful book, she wasn't given the proper credit. Through the choice of others, someone else's name appeared on the cover as the author. Ghostwriting didn't fit her personality.

Yet I have another friend who doesn't care whether she gets the credit for what she writes. "I just want the message to get out," she told me. "And if the only way it can reach the public is through the use of someone else's name, then I don't care. Some people have a message to share, but they don't have the talent to write it. The message is what is most important to me."

Not all of us are gifted in the area of serving, yet there are jobs that must be done. How do you handle the situation when it's a dirty job but somebody's got to do it?

Varying Approaches

Let's go back to the ever-popular church kitchen. For each of seven separate functions, seven differently gifted ladies were placed in charge of the kitchen. How will each one handle the job?

Administration took time to organize a committee, assign jobs, divide the kitchen into sections so the women wouldn't get in each other's way, and later reorganize the cupboards.

Mercy was so busy listening to the hurts and cares of the other ladies on the committee that she took hours to clean the kitchen.

Teaching had a running one-sided conversation with the other ladies, telling them about some interesting details of the lesson she was preparing for the following Sunday.

Encouraging went from lady to lady, comforting one, offering counsel to another, challenging a third one to start having a daily prayer time—all the while making everyone feel happy to be a part of the team.

Giving, noticing that the plates were cracked and the cups had broken handles, mentally decided she would replace them as a Christmas gift to the church.

Prophecy dazzled the kitchen crew with her latest story, making them laugh, but pressing her spiritual point as well. She settled a disagreement between two ladies, who both claimed the same pie pan, and instigated a lively debate over a controversial point in the pastor's sermon.

Serving bussed tables, stacked and washed the dishes, and carried out the garbage. As the last of her committee members went home, she packed the decorations and stored them for the next year. On her way out the door, hours after everyone else had left, she scooped up the dirty tablecloths and took them home to launder.

Uses Today

The one gifted with serving has the ability to discern needs, using her talents and resources to relieve or support others in their ministries.

It would be impossible to list all the ways the gift of serving could be used today. A few are listed below. Take time to write in some other areas, too.

> Assisting Sunday-school teachers
> Helping with the church sound system
> Doing secretarial work
> Assisting in the resource room
> Doing custodial work
> Volunteering to take meals to shut-ins
> Helping in the kitchen
> Cooking
> Driving the church bus

Exploring the Possibilities

How do you begin to find out if serving is your special area of gift? You probably already know the answer after reading this chapter. All of us, whether we have this as one of our special gifts or not, can serve Christ right where we are. Look around you. Who needs help today? Is it your neighbor? A friend? A relative? Your pastor or Sunday-school teacher?

Is there a dusty corner that needs wiping? Are there people who need a ride to the store? Is there someone who needs a respite from an aging parent or a nursery full of babies? Use God's eyes to see the needs and plunge right in. Do what you can and leave the results to God. He knows what you have done. Just keep giving out those cups of cold water in the name of Jesus.

What we do in the name of Jesus brings fruitfulness to the body of Christ. Our task is to remain in Christ and leave the harvest to Him.

"I am the vine," Jesus said; "you are the branches. If

a man remains in me and I in him, he will bear much fruit; apart from me you can do nothing" (John 15:5).

Promises to Claim

"Therefore, since through God's mercy we have this ministry, we do not lose heart" (2 Cor. 4:1).

"His master replied, 'Well done, good and faithful servant! . . . Come and share your master's happiness!' " (Matt. 25:21).

"The King will reply, 'I tell you the truth, whatever you did for one of the least of these brothers of mine, you did for me' " (Matt. 25:40).

For Further Study

Matt. 20:26–28; 24:45–47; 25:34–40; John 13:1–17; Acts 6:1–7; Col. 4:17; 2 Tim. 4:5; Heb. 1:14.

Questions to Ponder

1. How often do you willingly set aside your own plans in order to take care of other people's immediate needs?
2. Is your hands-on work for the Lord and others done cheerfully or grudgingly?
3. Would you rather cook a meal and deliver it to a shut-in or donate the money so someone else could do it?
4. In what way are you currently serving?

YOUR SONS & DAUGHTERS WILL PROPHESY

CHAPTER NINE

The sanctuary was darkened on this Easter Sunday morning. It was the last performance of the Easter week drama and Shari stood alert, watching for the choir director's cue. Off-stage a male voice intoned, "Early on Sunday morning Mary Magdalene went to the tomb . . ."

The music started and Shari quickly directed a blue-clad young woman down the side aisle. Shari dashed around the stairs and scurried into position behind the cardboard tomb. From there, undetected, she could prompt in case of forgotten lines.

In college Shari majored in drama, and when she became a Christian, she was delighted to use her skills in sharing the message of her new-found faith. This was the third year she had directed an adult Easter pageant, and each year the audience grew. This pleased Shari because more and more people were experiencing a gospel presentation.

Shari has many talents, but she is highly gifted in the area of prophecy. She has a compelling urgency to share the message of Christ with as many people as possible, and drama is her avenue.

Biblical Definition

"If a man's gift is prophesying, let him use it in proportion to his faith" (Rom. 12:6).

Propheteia is the Greek word here, but it is difficult to define. One source says it means "prediction," and another one says it means "to speak forth." The root word carries the meaning, "to consider in advance" and "to look out for beforehand." Dictionaries are sometimes confusing because there can be several definitions to one word; therefore the reader must make her own selection.

But to me, the clearest definition comes from Thayer's Greek lexicon. Thayer says prophecy is divinely inspired words that declare the purposes of God through three areas: reproof, comfort, and revelation.

I like that! It doesn't limit a prophecy-gifted person to only one area. It allows God to speak through this person to all of us in whatever way we need to hear. "But everyone who prophesies speaks to men for their strengthening, encouragement and comfort" (1 Cor. 14:3).

This gift *isn't* fortune-telling! Scripture clearly shows that fortune-telling is opposed to the truth about Jesus. Paul and Silas were so irritated by a fortune-telling spirit that they cast it out of a slave girl.

> We were met by a slave girl who had a spirit by which she predicted the future. She earned a great deal of money for her owners by fortune-telling. . . . Paul became so troubled that he turned around and said to the spirit, "In the name of Jesus Christ I command you to

come out of her!" At that moment the spirit left her. (Acts 16:16–18)

The one gifted with prophecy does not speak these words on her own, but rather tells the listener what God has revealed to her. Revelations are not mystical utterances from the cosmos but are based solidly on the Word of God and expressed according to the prophet's relationship with God.

Of course, God doesn't sling His words around carelessly. Nor did He leave us at the mercy of any who claim to be God's spokesmen. God established a test so we can recognize those who are actually sharing God's truth with us.

Prophets—True or False?

The Old Testament test of a prophet was accuracy. (See Deut. 18:20–22.) The penalty for an inaccurate revelation from God was death! No second chance.

How can we know today if a prophet isn't telling the truth?

> Do not believe every spirit, but test the spirits to see whether they are from God, because many false prophets have gone out into the world. This is how you can recognize the Spirit of God: Every spirit that acknowledges that Jesus Christ has come in the flesh is from God, but every spirit that does not acknowledge Jesus is not from God. (1 John 4:1–3)

We can test the spirits by using God's plumb line, His revelation to us, the Bible. God's Word says the prophet must acknowledge that Jesus Christ has come in the flesh. The true prophet does not simply acknowledge a good man named Jesus Christ, but rather Jesus, God's Son, the Christ—the Messiah!

If someone tells you something, which he says is a message from God, don't just sit there and accept it. Check it out for yourself. Find out what Scripture says. Are his words in complete agreement with the entire Word of God, or is he picking and choosing verses that seem to support his message, leaving out parts that don't fit and adding what he wants you to believe in words that sound like Scripture?

For example, someone might say to you, "God is love. Because He is love, He wants us all to go to heaven. A loving God would never condemn anyone to hell. Therefore, as long as we live lives filled with love and do good, we'll all go to heaven."

At first it sounds good. God is love. That's true. And it's also true that He wants us all to go to heaven. But then the accuracy falters. Although God is love, He insists that the only way to heaven is through confession of sin and acceptance of the substitutionary death of Christ.

> I tell you the truth, unless a man is born again, he cannot see the kingdom of God. (John 3:3)
> Jesus answered, "I am the way and the truth and the life. No one comes to the Father except through me." (John 14:6)
> If we confess our sins, he is faithful and just and will forgive us our sins and purify us from all unrighteousness. (1 John 1:9)

Even if we fill our lives with love and do all the good we can, we are still condemned to eternal hell if we do not follow God's truth as laid out for us in the whole Bible. Knowing the truth of God's Word will help us detect the inaccuracy of any who falsely claim to be speaking God's truth. Then we can stand firm and not be caught in the whirlpool of false teaching.

The believers in Berea followed this example when Paul came to them with the news about Jesus. They "examined the Scriptures every day to see if what Paul said was true" (Acts 17:11).

Biblical Examples

On the day of Pentecost, when the crowds were wondering what was happening and why all these men were speaking in strange languages, Peter, a contemporary prophet, stood and gave an accurate explanation based on scripture. "Fellow Jews and all of you who are in Jerusalem, let me explain this to you. . . ." He told the people that these events were the fulfillment of the prophet Joel's predictions about the coming of the Messiah (Jesus). (See Acts 2:14–32.)

Peter's words were divinely inspired, and he was speaking forth, revealing the hidden things of God. His words were also reproof for the wicked and comfort for those who yearned for a knowledge of God.

God didn't weave this gift only into the lives of men like Peter. There were others, too. Both men and women were gifted in the area of prophecy. Acts 2:17 says we will see a resurgence of this gift among men and women in the latter days. That means *we* (not only those who prophesied in New Testament times) can expect a fresh pouring forth of the Holy Spirit.

The inspired pen of Dr. Luke gives recognition to some New Testament people gifted with prophecy.

Men: Barnabas, Simeon, Lucius, Manaen, Saul (Acts 13:1), Judas, and Silas (Acts 15:32).

Women: Anna (Luke 2:36–38) and the four daughters of Philip (Acts 21:9).

Judas and Silas spent their time encouraging and strengthening the brothers. Nowhere does Scripture say they were foretelling the future.

Anna was an elderly woman who never left the temple

but worshiped night and day, fasting and praying. When Mary and Joseph came to the temple to present Jesus to the Lord, Anna immediately recognized God's revelation in the baby Jesus and began telling others about it.

I wonder if we recognize some of the gentle souls in our local churches who are listening to God?

Her name isn't Anna, but it might as well be. Della is a delightful elderly lady who loves the Lord. Her steel gray hair is pulled back in a knot at the nape of her neck, and she squints through wire-rimmed glasses. Her gnarled fingers caress the fragile pages of her well-worn Bible as she sits and listens closely to the pastor or Sunday-school teacher.

This modern-day Anna is always ready to give an explanation of God's Word. Is there a scripture verse that someone doesn't understand? Della can explain it. Is there a question about Christian living or confusion about which way God would want someone to act? She can clarify it. In her own gentle, quiet way, she is quick to back up her explanations with Scripture, quick to show us how God would have us think and live. She is a woman of prayer, a woman whose ears are finely tuned to the voice of God.

We hear only once about the four daughters of Philip. They must have been special women for Luke to mention them. Their work must have been notable and important, yet we never hear about them again.

The Controversy About Women

It has been frustrating for the daughters of God to have such a gift as prophecy, to be compelled to share the news of God, while many sincere Christians hold that a woman may not speak to the church. Our American Christian culture, for the most part, expects pastors to be men yet readily sends women to the mission field, expecting them to be the major spiritual leaders of their area. This seems to be a double standard!

Some churches, running the gamut from very evangelical to liberal, do believe God has given the gift of prophecy to both men and women. Today, therefore, more and more opportunities exist for women to express this gift. In a spirit of servanthood, women can step into those openings when God provides them.

Recently our local newspaper ran an article about women who work as pastors in our town. Several churches have such women on staff and one has a woman as its only pastor. But this is not a new phenomenon; the first pastor of my conservative, evangelical church was a woman, and in the course of seventy-five years other women have served there. God knows His children. He knows who is listening to Him and who can be used. Are you willing to let Him use you if He asks?

Heidi lives in a small farming town and struggled for a long time with her known gift of prophecy. There seemed to be few opportunities for her to use it, even though it was the largest blossom in her bouquet of spiritual gifts. For a number of years she attended a Bible study in a nearby city, taking all of the training she could get.

Finally, God opened a door for Heidi to start a Bible study group in a small community near her town. Once a week she traveled more than thirty miles to lead a Bible class of nearly fifty women. Through bad winter weather, hot summer sun, and dusty harvest season, Heidi kept her commitment, sharing the gospel with women who otherwise would have no regular Bible class. It has been a blessing both to the women and to Heidi for her to spread the gospel in this manner. When we are willing, God will provide the opening.

A prophet also makes the meaning of Scripture clear. Someone with this gift might contribute in a Sunday school class, saying, "This verse means . . ." and they translate it into today's culture and words. They know how to apply scriptural truths to our daily lives.

When prophets see a disturbing situation, they are not afraid to confront someone with God's truth. One gifted with prophecy will openly ask, "Are you living up to God's standards in this area?" It takes someone with a strong will to be able to confront others firmly with the truth.

This is in complete contrast to a mercy-gifted person who is unable to confront others. Those gifted with prophecy see everything as black and white. When they point out blind spots and gray areas in other people's lives, they don't do it to be critical. They simply want to be right, and they want others to be right, too.

If someone disagrees with her, the one gifted with prophecy will stand firm. She won't back down. In fact, she will thoroughly enjoy comparing her beliefs with others and pointing out why the others are wrong. This is usually a straight-forward debate rather than a mealy-mouthed discussion. Reproof comes from an overpowering drive to share God's truth with the listener.

The prophecy-gifted person is also keenly sensitive to the Holy Spirit. God can reveal things to her because she is discerning. She knows what is and what is not God's truth. And, knowing God's truth, she won't hesitate to share it.

As with all the other gifts, prophecy has its characteristic joys and sorrows. Think of some people you know with these identifying characteristics as you read through the list.

Characteristic Joys

1. She has the ability to spot a phony before others do.

2. For her, everything is either black or white. There are no gray areas, especially where sin is concerned.

3. She needs outward evidence in someone's life to prove his or her inward heart change.

4. She enjoys a lively debate and has the courage to stand firm even if no one else stands with her.

5. She has an inner drive to communicate the truth of Scripture to everyone.

6. She usually has a direct, frank approach and is able to persuade people, especially when God's Word is involved.

7. She likes to show people where their blind spots are and wants others to point out hers.

8. She has an urgency to reveal sin and proclaim God's truth, whether in a group or one to one.

9. If she clearly understands God's will in a matter, she doesn't hesitate to make it known to others.

Characteristic Cautions

1. She may seem stubborn because she has a strong will.

2. She has strong opinions and doesn't like compromise.

3. She may seem insensitive and doesn't like to display emotions, especially in public.

4. She may use showmanship if it helps get her point across.

In seeking to identify people with the gift of prophecy, look for someone who has confidence and authority, someone who can withstand stress, pain, or persecution while proclaiming God's truth. This person may also have a tendency to exaggerate and dramatize in order to press her point.

The one gifted with prophecy recognizes truth in God's Word and is compelled to do something about it.

If You Score Low in Prophecy

If you are extremely low in prophecy, you may sometimes excuse a person's sin or make light of it when that person really needs to be confronted with it and confess it. You may find gray areas confusing and become irritated with those who see everything as black or white.

If you don't have this gift, you may be tempted to claim it anyway because it carries so much weight. Saying "God told me . . ." gets people's attention. The church can be caught in a power play, a struggle to see who can gain the most authority in the eyes of others.

The gift of prophecy is perhaps the most abused in our contemporary church. Some people want this gift so badly that they try to fake it, but a prophecy-gifted person can quickly spot a phony.

"Verses of Scripture don't leap off the page at me like they do to you," a friend told me. "I'd like to be able to share God's truth with others, but I'm never sure that what I'm saying is His special message to my listeners."

There are times when we are in a position to help others understand God's message, but we don't feel qualified. If prophecy isn't one of your major gifts, how do you handle these situations? Perhaps you are a Sunday-school teacher or a women's Bible study leader, or maybe you are the only person in your private world who is a Christian. If someone asks a spiritual question, what do you do?

The best plan of all is to be prepared. This is one of

those unique areas that can be learned, but it takes hard work. Begin with your own basic Bible study. Memorize Scripture according to subject so if a specific question is asked, you'll be able to quote exactly the right verse. You can't go wrong if you offer God's Word as your answer.

Take advantage of classes and books available that teach you how to proclaim God's Word. There are printed sermons suitable for almost any occasion, ready for use. Your local Christian bookstore is loaded with Bible study books. Ask for trusted and reliable authors. Many Christian authors are gifted in prophecy; make use of their material.

Learn from a prophecy-gifted person. If a situation falls into what you perceive to be a gray area, ask questions of someone who has the prophecy gift so you'll know how to advise another person.

If You Score High in Prophecy

If you score high in prophecy, learn to temper your boldness with mercy. To others you may sometimes appear to be very harsh and dogmatic. Having the knowledge of God's truth, you may tend to plow people down like a bulldozer. Also, be careful that your showmanship doesn't overpower your message. If all your audience sees is the entertainment, they have missed the real message.

You may tend to be extremist and impulsive. The person gifted with prophecy is able to bring people to personal accountability and cause them to change, but beware of being overly critical and correcting others in a wrong way. Ask the Lord for a special portion of sensitivity and gentleness.

If you tend to see the one thing that's wrong and overlook the nine things that are right, remember to encourage the good while correcting the bad. Though you may appear tough on the outside, you probably love deeply and are completely loyal. Don't be afraid to show it.

People look to prophecy-gifted people for their spiritual standards, so guard against pride, and don't drive yourself crazy trying to be the "perfect" saint.

Varying Approaches

Dianne is expressing her gift of prophecy through writing for Christian publications. Her spiritual insights in print have brought comfort and encouragement to many people. She also is a photographer and takes pictures that add depth and meaning to her articles, visually communicating the messages of God.

Another example of one who uses her gift of prophecy is Pat, who frequently speaks about her faith at banquets, meetings, and women's retreats. Fortunately for both of these women, they have found an open field that allows them to express God's gift of prophecy in their lives.

But not every person gifted with prophecy ministers in an up-front position. Rhonda is a quiet woman who would be extremely uncomfortable in the spotlight. But her gift of prophecy is just as valuable.

Rhonda often is prompted by God to give a word of comfort or encouragement to people around her. She will slip her arm around a shoulder and speak words of comfort at the most important times. People say, "It was as though her words came directly from the mouth of God. She said exactly what I needed to hear."

Uses Today

The one gifted with prophecy has the ability to proclaim the truth of God's Word under the inspiration of the Holy Spirit, bringing conviction to the hearer.

How does this gift fit into the body of Christ today?

The body of Christ needs people who will boldly proclaim God's truth. If we don't proclaim it, how will others know what God's truth really is? The body needs God's revelation through the power of the Holy Spirit. The body also needs someone who can interpret God's truth and relate it to life.

This gift clearly identifies sin, discerns what is truth and what isn't, and recognizes cults—keeping us on God's pathway.

How can this gift be used?

Teaching
Preaching
Serving as a missionary
Writing
Serving as a board member
Participating in drama
Counseling
Witnessing
Serving in any form of communication (film, photos, art, discussions, public speaking)

Add other people or positions that need to have the gift of prophecy.

Exploring the Possibilities

Is this one of the major flowers in your bouquet? If it is, how can you seek to bloom? As always, begin on your knees. Ask God to open an area (of His choosing) in which you can use this gift.

Are you involved in a Sunday school class or Bible study group? Be willing to assist the teacher in clarifying God's message to the group. Maybe God is asking you to step out and be the leader of such a class. Now is the time to follow His guidance.

Look at your skills. Are you a photographer? Then take photos that convey a spiritual message. Are you a writer? Communicate God's message on the blank page in front of you. Are you a speaker? Declare His truth to the audiences He provides. Are you an actress or have drama training? Get involved in Christian drama.

Promise to Claim

"He who prophesies edifies the church" (1 Cor. 14:4).

For Further Study

Joel 2:28; Matt. 7:22; Acts 2:17; 1 Cor. 13:2, 8–9; 14:4–5; 1 Thess. 5:20; 2 Pet. 1:20; Rev. 11:18–19.

Questions to Ponder

1. Do tears spring easily to your eyes? Is it an embarrassment for you to let them show in public?
2. When was the last time you sensed God showing you His special insight in a situation when others weren't quite clear on the subject? Does this happen often in your life?
3. Because of a compelling, inner urgency, how often do you find yourself sharing God's truth with others, especially if it concerns an area of sin?
4. If someone tells you he is a Christian, do you accept it on face value or do you wait for confirmation in his life?

UNIQUELY YOU

CHAPTER TEN

At last it's time to put all that you've learned in the previous nine chapters to work.

You could hurry through this evaluation in only a few minutes, but you would be cheating yourself. Please take your time. As you read each statement, pray about it. Ask the Holy Spirit to help you with every one. Perhaps even take a few days to work on it slowly.

One of the things I've learned is that the evaluation may change slightly according to the type of day you are having. If you are tired or have a headache or are under some kind of stress, your evaluations may not be as accurate as they might be otherwise. If you are relaxed, rested, and comfortable, your evaluation of each statement will better reflect the real you.

Like a child at Christmas, the anticipation is exciting!

DISCOVERY EVALUATION

Read each statement through carefully and evaluate yourself on a scale of 0 to 5.

0 = doesn't describe me at all
1 = not very much
2 = occasionally
3 = sometimes
4 = usually
5 = describes me fully

_____ 1. I have the ability to perceive and set long-range goals and make specific plans to achieve them.

_____ 2. I thoroughly enjoy counseling other people.

_____ 3. I love research and checking information, words and their definitions.

_____ 4. I have the ability to see needs other people don't notice.

_____ 5. I am sensitive to the emotional needs of others; I seem to know when they are hurting.

_____ 6. I am practical and short-term goals catch my interest.

_____ 7. I can spot a phony before other people discern one.

_____ 8. I am an organizer. I can take a series of tasks, organize them properly and help others to get organized, too.

_____ 9. I view problems as an opportunity for spiritual growth.

_____ 10. It is extremely important to me that words be used correctly.

_____ 11. I prefer to meet needs quietly without publicity.

_____ 12. I seem to be attracted to anyone who is in distress.

_____ 13. I am quickly aware of practical needs.

_____ 14. Everything is either black or white to me; there are no gray areas, especially where sin is concerned.

_____ 15. I can take a large job and easily break it down into minute details in order to reach a specific goal.

_____ 16. I am able to define positive steps for solving a problem or meeting a need.

_____ 17. It's easy for me to gather, organize, and retain a large amount of facts.

_____ 18. I can find great bargains, and any purchase I make is a wise one.

_____ 19. I have a deep desire to ease pain and to bring healing.

_____ 20. I enjoy being involved in hands-on projects.

_____ 21. I need outward evidence in a person's life to prove his inward heart change.

_____ 22. I can coordinate people and things (whatever it takes) to accomplish long-range goals.

_____ 23. I love to make practical applications for everyday life from Scripture.

_____ 24. I have a logical, objective approach to life.

_____ 25. Others follow my giving and give to my projects.

_____ 26. Prayer is a very important part of my life, even more so than many of my Christian friends.

_____ 27. I seem to have an extra measure of physical stamina.

_____ 28. I enjoy a lively debate and have the courage to stand firm on my beliefs even if I stand alone.

_____ 29. It's easy for me to delegate responsibility to other people.

_____ 30. I have the ability to verbally comfort the hurting.

_____ 31. I have to know the authority behind information. It bothers me when an illustration is used out of context.

_____ 32. I don't want to just give to a project; I want to be somewhat involved with the project, too.

_____ 33. I seem to know instinctively when people have sincere motives.

_____ 34. I am strongly motivated to complete any task I do. In fact, I readily look for shortcuts to get the job done quickly and efficiently.

_____ 35. I have an inner drive to communicate the truth of Scripture to everyone.

_____ 36. Pressure is my friend. In fact, pressure helps me get the job done, and I usually strive to finish it ahead of schedule.

_____ 37. I enjoy challenging the spiritually apathetic to grow in the Lord.

_____ 38. If someone comes to me with a problem, I would rather help her discover her own solution than give her a simple answer.

_____ 39. I don't like to be pressured into giving.

_____ 40. I can often see things from the other person's point of view; and when she talks to me, I actually *feel* her situation, often crying with her.

_____ 41. I would gladly inconvenience myself in order to help others, and I have a negative reaction to people who aren't willing to get involved.

_____ 42. Even with my direct, frank approach, I seem to be able to persuade people to my point of view, especially when God's Word is involved.

_____ 43. If there is a need, I can easily coordinate everything necessary to meet that need.

_____ 44. I enjoy being around other people.

_____ 45. I try to give detailed instructions to others so they will be able to follow exactly what I say.

_____ 46. What some people may see as selfishness is actually my personal thriftiness.

_____ 47. I receive a blessing from visiting hospitals, jails, nursing homes, or those who are shut-ins.

_____ 48. I'm involved in a number of activities and projects.

_____ 49. I don't like compromise and I have very strong opinions.

_____ 50. Most people can't keep up with me when I'm involved in a project. I push hard to reach my goals.

_____ 51. I am more interested in the essence rather than detail, so I may take some things out of context in order to press a point.

_____ 52. Learning new information is important to me, and I always want to know more.

_____ 53. I prefer any gift I give to have long-range value, not just meet an immediate need.

_____ 54. Working with the people who are ignored by others brings a special joy to me.

_____ 55. I believe that doing things cheerfully is one way to show my love.

_____ 56. People may think I am insensitive because I don't like to display my emotions in public.

_____ 57. I'm a project person. To me, getting the job done is more important than the individual people who are involved.

_____ 58. I want the people I counsel to overcome their problems so much that I sometimes get more involved in working out a solution than the counselee himself.

_____ 59. Finding the exact illustration that will add meaning to my instruction is important to me.

_____ 60. I don't like to be in debt to anyone for any reason.

_____ 61. I'd rather be around other people than be alone.

_____ 62. I am known as a good worker and willingly do whatever task needs doing.

_____ 63. I can show people where their blind spots are, and I want them to point out mine.

_____ 64. I'm not as sensitive to the needs of other people as I'd like to be. Often I don't see their hurts.

_____ 65. I can see what people can become with God's help, and I want to help them get there.

_____ 66. I find myself constantly correcting people around me. People sometimes say I'm too critical.

_____ 67. I don't mind living at a lower standard than my friends because it allows me to give more to God's work.

_____ 68. I have difficulty confronting people directly because I can't stand to hurt anyone either with words or actions. Consequently, others may view me as weak and indecisive.

_____ 69. I am a good follower and am very flexible.

_____ 70. I feel that a little showmanship doesn't hurt if it helps get my point across.

_____ 71. I tend to treat people the same way they treat me.

_____ 72. I hurt when others are hurting, and I want to help them turn to God for their answers.

_____ 73. Whenever I tell a story or pass along some information, I try to include all the details, no matter how small. I feel that details add depth of meaning.

_____ 74. Money management is easy for me, and I appear to do it well.

_____ 75. I can easily be hurt by the words and actions of others, which sometimes cause me to be depressed.

_____ 76. I have been known to let people take advantage of me.

_____ 77. Some people think I'm stubborn because I have a very strong will.

_____ 78. People sometimes see me as being bossy. I have to be careful not to be too pushy.

_____ 79. I enjoy changing people's attitudes from negative to positive whenever they are around me.

_____ 80. I don't take anything anyone says on face value. I need to know the _whys_ as well as where the information came from.

_____ 81. For some reason I seem to be able to acquire money easily.

_____ 82. I seem to lack the ability to be firm and can't make decisions under stress.

_____ 83. Spiritual things tend to get lost in my focus on practical things.

_____ 84. It is very important to me to reveal sin and proclaim God's truth whether in a group or one to one.

_____ 85. I'm nit-picky about any job. Details are very important to me.

_____ 86. Even if someone has taken a nose-dive, I encourage her to get up and try again.

_____ 87. When I research something, I love to share that knowledge with others.

_____ 88. I don't give out of a sense of duty; giving money or things to God brings me deep pleasure, and I do it cheerfully.

_____ 89. I am more emotional than others around me, and I know my emotions affect the way I act.

_____ 90. Others may see me as a pushy person, but I just want to get the work done.

_____ 91. When I have a clear understanding of God's will, I don't hesitate to make it known to others.

Place each evaluation score in the appropriate box on the next page. Add the numbers in the boxes and place the total at the end of each line.

FINDING A MINISTRY YOU CAN LOVE

Add each column down and place total on the line below.

1.	2.	3.	4.	5.	6.	7.
8.	9.	10.	11.	12.	13.	14.
15.	16.	17.	18.	19.	20.	21.
22.	23.	24.	25.	26.	27.	28.
29.	30.	31.	32.	33.	34.	35.
36.	37.	38.	39.	40.	41.	42.
43.	44.	45.	46.	47.	48.	49.
50.	51.	52.	53.	54.	55.	56.
57.	58.	59.	60.	61.	62.	63.
64.	65.	66.	67.	68.	69.	70.
71.	72.	73.	74.	75.	76.	77.
78.	79.	80.	81.	82.	83.	84.
85.	86.	87.	88.	89.	90.	91.

1)_____ 2)_____ 3)_____ 4)_____ 5)_____ 6)_____ 7)_____

1) Administration   4) Giving   7) Prophesying
2) Encouraging   5) Mercy
3) Teaching   6) Serving

You probably had one or two scores that were higher than all the rest, while others fell into recognizable clusters. Remember, the higher score indicates how much of that gift you see in yourself. Circle the very top one (or two or three) and write them here:

1. _____

2. _____

3. _____

When I took this evaluation, my scores indicated that one gift was quite a bit stronger than all the rest. Close behind, two almost tied. After a large drop in scores, the others were scattered further down the line.

Now you know the basic structure for your spiritual gifts bouquet. Are you surprised? Go back and compare these results with what you wrote in answer to the questions at the end of the first chapter. Are they similar? At the back of this book, there are two copies of the evaluation you just filled out. Appendix A and B are for two other people to use in evaluating you. One of them might be your spouse. Another could be a close friend. It's important to see how others view us. Their opinions may help us adjust our own evaluations.

Ask your evaluators to be candid in their answers. When they have completed their appraisals, pour them a cup of tea and have a heart-to-heart discussion about their answers. You may discover something entirely new about yourself, something you didn't dream was even there. Don't close your mind to what they say. Their opinions may be the beginning of a whole new avenue of serving the Lord.

In each of the previous chapters I've given you some

joys and cautions to consider, and this chapter is no different.

Characteristic Joys

We have discovered all the parts of a glorious bouquet to grace your life, and now we can begin putting those things together.

The precious pinks of Mercy and the bright yellows of Serving are gathered next to the brilliant blues of Prophecy. The sparkling white of Administration is offset by the deep purples of Giving, while golden Encouraging is nestled next to glowing red Teaching.

Everywhere around you are baskets of hopeful greens. Hope is the background for all we do in Christ. Hope is like one TV commercial's claim for hairspray—it keeps on going even when you quit.

The Apostle Paul wrote to Titus about hope. He said that "the grace of God . . . teaches us . . . to live . . . godly lives . . . while we wait for the blessed hope—the glorious appearing of our great God and Savior, Jesus Christ" (Titus 2:11–13). Titus was to keep on serving while he waited for the second coming of Christ—that's our hope. All that we do is based on the hope of the return of Christ.

Even when the waiting seems long, the difficulties seem overwhelming, and the serving seems endless, "let us hold unswervingly to the hope we profess, for he who promised is faithful" (Heb. 10:23).

Sometimes Christ's second coming appears to be a long way off, but God has promised it will happen, and we can hold on to that hope in faith. "Now faith is being sure of what we hope for and certain of what we do not see" (Heb. 11:1). Let the greens of hope fill all the gaps in your bouquet of spiritual gifts.

Characteristic Cautions

First, the discovery sheet isn't perfect (although I wish it could be). Taking this evaluation won't miraculously change your life. Use it as a guideline. Allow the Holy Spirit to speak to you and let it become a springboard for new thoughts and ideas.

Second, don't try to use this evaluation with children or new Christians. In my opinion, neither have had enough time or experience to get an accurate reading. Remember, you can't pick a bouquet when the plant has only sprouted.

In the next chapter we'll talk about some areas in which you can use your spiritual gifts to serve God and build up the body of Christ.

WHERE DO I FIT IN THE BODY OF CHRIST?

CHAPTER ELEVEN

Well, are you excited? Did you learn something new about yourself? How did your evaluation compare with the ones your spouse or friends did?

If your scores were consistently low or extremely close together, don't worry. Some people tend to answer the statements conservatively while others respond in extremes. I had a lot of zeros and fives, so my scores were widely separated. But several of my friends used basically twos, threes, and a few fours. Their scores were low and tightly clustered. With this system, it doesn't matter. The results are the same.

I was surprised at my personal results when I did this evaluation, but looking back, I shouldn't have been. God had woven these traits into my life from the beginning, and they were already at work. Finding out who I am and what God has created in me was a big relief. Now I'm far more conscious of where I work and what I do. I avoid being put in a place where I feel extremely uncomfortable or unfulfilled.

What's next? First, go back to the chapters that correspond with your top evaluation scores. Scan them now with yourself in mind. Concentrate on the principles given and determine where you fit.

Andrea discovered she was gifted in encouragement and administration. One of the things she did naturally was talk to people and counsel them. As she prayed about where she fit in the body of Christ, the Lord gave her a special concern for pregnant girls. Wherever Andrea went in her community, she became more and more aware of young women, both married and unmarried, who were having difficulty in their lives because they were pregnant. Andrea wanted to help.

Eventually she was able to form a local chapter of an organization that provided testing, counseling, and financial and spiritual support for pregnant women. Andrea opened an office, gathered materials, found resources, contacted doctors and community service people. When her first advertisement appeared in the newspaper, the phone began to ring.

Her heart reached out to those who called, women and young girls who were afraid they were pregnant and didn't know where to turn. Some were considering abortion. Others needed a place to live or food supplements. One woman Andrea visited was nearing time to give birth to her second child, yet her first child was sleeping in a cardboard box beside her bed! Andrea delighted in bringing a crib and clean sheets into that home.

Her stories move the hearts of her listeners as Andrea visits churches, explaining this special ministry. All of her work is done outside the church walls, yet she is actively and effectively serving the body of Christ with the gifts God has given to her.

How are *you* going to use the gifts God has woven into you? What form will *your* ministry take?

Let's say your major area of ministry is encouragement with a supporting ministry of mercy. Look at your natural talents and learned skills. We don't ignore these. We add them so they aren't wasted but become an enhancement to God's created gifts.

If your natural (God-given) talent is music, you can encourage the body of Christ by being part of the choir, singing solos (depending on your skill level), or playing an instrument. With your added mercy gift, you may choose to take your music ministry into nursing homes, hospitals, or the homes of shut-ins. You may also choose to use those talents in Sunday school, children's church, or a class for the handicapped.

The possible combinations of these two ministries multiplies infinitely under God's guidance. You can add to them by increasing your skill level. Take music lessons (vocal or instrumental). Study new music to constantly be aware of words that would encourage your listeners. If your area is instrumental, work with the song leader or vocalist to choose music that will blend with and enhance the message or lesson for that day.

Now let's change the situation slightly. You could have the same gift combination of encouragement/mercy, but your natural talent or learned skill might be *talking*.

We all know people with the "gift of gab." (Although I didn't find this listed as a spiritual gift in our Romans passage, some people seem to have an abundant supply!) In this instance you could be effective in counseling (beware of talking so much you forget to listen) and/or discipling. A Christian friend may need comfort and guidance. Perhaps you know some new Christians who need someone to help them grow.

You see, with the same combination of gifts, the focus

of ministry can be completely different. Here the skill level can be enhanced by taking classes or reading books on counseling and discipling.

It would be impossible to list all the gift/ministry combinations or even the unique opportunities there are for serving the body of Christ. However, some of the major categories can be classified according to the gifts. Remember, all the gifts can be used in each of these categories. You will simply approach the position in view of your gifts.

ADAPTING YOUR GIFTS TO
SPECIFIC MINISTRIES

Look at your cluster of gifts. If it helps you, draw a bouquet of various-sized flowers and label each blossom according to your score results. No gift is isolated from the rest. They all affect, enhance, and blend with one another.

As you search through these areas, prayerfully ask the Holy Spirit for guidance to show you where you fit in the body of Christ.

Administration

Performing clerical or secretarial tasks (taking attendance in Sunday school classes; taking minutes in a committee; assisting in church office); serving as committee chairman, project leader, resource room coordinator, wedding coordinator, board member, department head.

Teaching

Teaching Sunday school or in-home Bible classes, teaching Christian living/education classes, discipling, developing Christian education materials, pastoring, speaking, writing.

Encouraging

Discipling others, teaching Sunday school classes, counseling, pastoring, writing notes of encouragement, interceding for others in prayer, greeting people in the church foyer.

Giving

Supplying material resources, supporting church and missions projects, serving as a missionary, sharing your life through faith and encouragement, giving yourself to full-time Christian service.

Mercy

Visiting hospitals, rest homes, prisons; comforting; doing funeral follow-up; working with the handicapped; being part of a prayer chain; working in the church nursery; volunteering for a children's Sunday school grandparent program (staying with sick kids so parents can participate); assisting in any part of the Sunday school ministry; identifying and reporting to others when someone is in distress; working as a nurse or doctor.

Serving

Working in any type of technical service (photography, lighting, sound); helping the elderly; driving the church bus; ushering; assisting in office or resource room; cooking and serving meals; helping with the kitchen, property maintenance, custodial duties, hospitality, esthetics, ladies' calling group, social/fellowship events, bridal/baby showers.

Prophecy

Preaching, teaching Sunday school and Bible classes, serving as a missionary, participating in drama, discipling, teaching Christian education classes, assisting teachers in explaining biblical truth, writing, speaking.

Gifts, Ministries, and Change

As the needs of the body of Christ change, the focus of your ministry may change as well. Perhaps you've been involved in one spot for a long time and something happens to remove you from that area. Don't sit back and say, "I guess I'm not needed anymore" or, "I can't do anything else." That's nonsense! Your gifts haven't changed. God may simply want you to change your focus.

Ask Him to direct your attention to a new area where those same gifts can be used. It may involve a whole new way of thinking for you. It may require that you enhance your present skills or develop new ones, as Anita did.

"The past six months have been a difficult time of transition for me," Anita confessed. "I've been so active as director of the children's program that I couldn't think about anything else. But God seems to be asking me to do something so new, so wholly foreign, I have to be sure before I make the change."

We knew Anita had an administration/teaching/prophecy gift cluster, and God seemed to be directing her toward women's ministries. She had already been leading women's Bible study groups and doing some public speaking. But God was guiding her to let go of the children's program and wholeheartedly step into this new area.

We prayed together many times, and soon Anita felt God's assurance that He was leading in this direction. She answered His call to full-time Christian service. From then on, she was constantly being asked to speak at women's retreats, to teach Bible classes, and to counsel hurting women. She went back to school for some additional training, and eventually, Anita became an ordained minister. Currently she is working on staff at her church.

"It was scary at first when I started making the change," she admits, "but it has been worth every ounce of effort."

Why did God give us these gifts? Was it to glorify ourselves or Him? Eph. 4:12–13 says that the gifts were given "to prepare God's people for works of service, so that the body of Christ may be built up until we all reach unity in the faith and in the knowledge of the Son of God and become mature, attaining to the whole measure of the fullness of Christ."

We are to meet the needs of the body of Christ. That's why God gave those gifts to us.

Should you change what you are currently doing? I can't answer that for you. But as you seek the guidance of the Holy Spirit, prayerfully consider your current position and how it utilizes the gifts God has revealed that He has given to you. If you are functioning within the realm of your gifts, enhance them with increased skill.

If your gifts are not being best used in your current ministry and you've been feeling unfulfilled (or you aren't doing anything at all), prayerfully consider contacting a person in charge of a ministry in your gift range. Offer to be part of that ministry.

Please don't go to the pastor and say, "I've just taken a spiritual gifts evaluation, and now I want to be the church organist (soloist, choir director, secretary), so Mrs. Jones will have to step aside and let me do it!'' Maybe you know you could do the job better than Mrs. Jones, but remember, we all *fit into the body of Christ.*

Offer to be used and let God arrange exactly *where* and *when.* His timing is far better than ours. Our purpose isn't to hurt or replace others, but to blend together to enhance each other's ministries. We are to build up the body, not cause it pain. The Holy Spirit's control brings about a natural flow of change that best suits God's plans.

Can you sense the relief of the church's squeaking machinery as the oil of the Holy Spirit pours through it, moving gears and levers into their proper place? I can almost hear the groans lessen as the aches and pains of the body of Christ are relieved when we move into the ministries that use our God-given gifts.

Spiritual Gifts and Responsibility

"Since teaching isn't my gift," you say, "I don't have to do anything. Guess I'll just sit back and coast!" Wrong!

You may have been so shocked at the results that you don't want to do anything. Please don't quit at this point. Perhaps you think you couldn't possibly function in your high-scoring gifts. Lack of confidence may prevent you from receiving (and being) God's blessing.

What are your responsibilities?

If you feel insecure, an easy way to explore your newly discovered gifts is to apprentice yourself to one or more people who are successfully functioning in that area. Walk with them; learn from them in a low-key, nonthreatening manner.

How are you measuring up? Does your faith match your actions and activities? What are you going to do about it?

Explore, Examine, Evaluate

Now is the time to *explore* the possibilities of ministry. Stretch yourself and see where God leads you. Try things you've never done before. Don't limit yourself or God. He may start you down a "generic" path and suddenly send you off into a hidden lane where exquisite rare roses bloom.

Jean attended the classes I taught on finding and using your spiritual gifts. She discovered she had a teaching/mercy/serving blend. That pleased her because she had been active as a junior age Sunday-school teacher. Yet recently she had felt it was time to step aside for a while, and during that time she attended my classes.

An odd thing happened to her. Within a few weeks she was asked to become the coordinator for the entire adult Sunday school department. "But that's administration," she protested to me, "and administration is way down on my list. It really isn't one of my gifts." I agreed to pray with her for God's guidance while she made a decision.

A short time later she came back with her answer. "I'm to take the position anyway, even though it isn't my major gift."

It has been interesting to watch her work. She brought to the job her learned skill of organizing people, admitting openly that it wasn't her best area of service. But even better, she approached the position from the perspective of her gifts: teaching, mercy, and serving.

At that time, her local church needed a gentle, merciful director, not an overwhelming administrator. In just a few weeks the local body sensed a lessening of strain as the Holy Spirit poured His oil of love into that situation and the teachers learned to work together.

Be willing to explore an area, even if it isn't your gift.

That new position may need exactly what you can bring to it.

Next, *examine* your feelings. Do you sense an inner fulfillment, or are you frustrated? As you continue to explore new ministries, keep checking. God and the body of Christ will confirm to you whether or not you belong in that position, but your own persistent feelings of inadequacy and frustration may be another clue.

If I explored the possibility of playing the church organ, the body of Christ would quickly let me know that isn't my ministry. But when I step in front of a microphone to speak, or pick up a piece of chalk at a blackboard, or organize a committee, then the local body quickly affirms me, confirming the fulfillment I sense in these positions.

Finally, *evaluate* your effectiveness. There should be some positive results from what you are doing. If you aren't as effective as you should be, do you need more training? Is it time to change what you are doing? Do you need to expend more time and effort?

If your husband shares your spiritual beliefs, your effectiveness may increase if you know what his gifts are, too.

What are his gifts? List them here:

How do your gifts fit together with his?

The Matter of Viewpoint

To show you how we view each other differently, let's compare two couples who tested each other.

Jan sees her gifts as teaching/prophesying/serving, but her husband, Roy, views hers as teaching/encouraging/administration. He placed serving and prophesying at the bottom of his list for her. I tend to agree with her husband's view of her, and so did several people who attend her church.

On the other hand, Roy sees his gifts as teaching/mercy/serving. Jan agreed with the teaching, but put serving and administration next on her list for him. Mercy was fourth from the top. It's interesting that I also agree with Jan's view of her husband rather than his evaluation.

The second couple also perceived each other differently. Martin sees his gifts as prophecy/encouraging/giving, and Lydia comes close to his evaluation. She says his are prophecy/encouraging/ teaching. Giving was fifth on her evaluation for him.

Lydia perceives her gifts as mercy/encouraging/giving, while Martin views hers as giving/teaching/encouraging. Mercy was fifth on his list for her. This time I agree with Lydia's view of herself. She displays a great deal of mercy in her life.

Both couples have spent a considerable amount of time discussing their views of each other. They say it has helped them adjust better in their marriages. Jan says, "Instead of trying to change Roy, I now know that some of these traits are special things God has given to him. God needs him to be that way, and I can plan ahead, knowing how Roy will react."

Martin and Lydia have noticed that because he has such a strong prophecy gift and mercy was at the very bottom, he needs her mercy gift to balance his life. And she needs his strong prophecy to balance the extremes of her mercy. Both have said they now have changed the way they discipline their daughter.

After Martin strongly reacted to something their

daughter had done, he said to his wife, "Oh, *that's* why I came on so strong. It's a trait of prophecy."

"Yes," she agreed, "and now mercy is going to have to go and fix it."

Because they are learning about each other, they can help temper the cautions of their gifts and enhance the joys. Recently, after services at the church where Martin is senior pastor, he asked Lydia, "Did Prophecy do OK today, or did I come on too strong?"

"Maybe a bit strong," she replied (mercy), "but that was a message we all needed to hear (encouraging), and the only way it can be said is strongly."

Working together, husbands and wives can blend their gifts for a more effective ministry to the body of Christ.

If you are married, also consider which type of relational group your husband fits into. (See Chapter 2.) Is it the same as yours? If not, how different are the two groups into which you fit? And how will the differences affect the type of Christian service you do?

These same questions are applicable to any family or living situation, not just husband/wife combination. We need to be aware of the gifts and comfort zones for people who closely surround us.

I seem to work well in front of a large group, but my husband is most comfortable in a small, familiar group. Instead of each struggling to make the other fit into his or her plans, we are learning to allow each other to be different.

I love to get lots of people together for parties or family occasions, but I'm learning to plan some small group situations for my husband. To force him to always adapt to an uncomfortable situation is unfair.

As you become more and more familiar with these seven spiritual gifts and learn how they function in the body of Christ, you'll be able to help others find where they fit, too. This could be a very important function for you in your local area.

There are so many daughters of God serving in quiet desperation, frustrated and unfulfilled. Think what a relief, what a joy, what a release it could be to your friends to find a more perfect place to serve Christ. Ask God to help you become part of this plan for causing the spiritual body to grow.

Do It!

It isn't enough to just learn about spiritual gifts and avenues for joyous Christian service. We have to *do* what God commands us to do.

Scripture teaches that we can show our love to God by obeying Him. "If you love me, you will obey what I command" (John 14:15). Read the rest of that chapter (John 14:15–31). At the end, Jesus provides the greatest example for us to follow. He says, "The world must learn that I love the Father and that I do exactly what my Father has commanded me" (v. 31).

Jesus himself was involved in doing, not just learning. His purpose for coming was to be used by the Father in whatever way the Father commanded. Our purpose is the same, to be used of God.

To sit back and never change or do anything becomes disobedience. But if we plunge in, we can have a part in the fascinating, exciting, vibrant body of Christ.

There's a fresh wind blowing in the ranks of the Christian women. Are you there, allowing your Father to use you, seeking to serve Him in joy?

Promises to Claim

If I step out in faith, will God let me down?

The one who calls you is faithful and he will do it. (1 Thess. 5:24)

*How can I know for sure just where God is leading me?
I can see the first step but I don't know where I'll go from
there.*

I will lead the blind by ways they have not known,
along unfamiliar paths I will guide them; I will turn the
darkness into light before them and make the rough
places smooth. These are the things I will do; I will not
forsake them. (Isaiah 42:16)

*What will people think if I try something different?
Will they laugh at me or reject me?*

So we say with confidence, "The Lord is my helper;
I will not be afraid. What can man do to me?" (Heb. 13:6)

Will I succeed or fail if I begin a new ministry?

Jesus replied, "I tell you the truth, if you have faith
and do not doubt, not only can you do what was done
to the fig tree, but also you can say to this mountain,
'Go, throw yourself into the sea,' and it will be done."
(Matt. 21:21)

How do I handle my fear of all the unknowns?

So do not fear, for I am with you; do not be dismayed,
for I am your God. I will strengthen you and help you;
I will uphold you with my righteous right hand. (Isa.
41:10)

For Further Study

Matt. 25:14–30; Mark 16:3–4 (imaginary hindrances to
Christian workers); 1 Cor. 12; Eph. 4:16; 1 Pet. 4:10.

APPENDIX A

DISCOVERY EVALUATION

Read each statement through carefully and evaluate yourself on a scale of 0 to 5.

0 = doesn't describe me at all
1 = not very much
2 = occasionally
3 = sometimes
4 = usually
5 = describes me fully

_____ 1. I have the ability to perceive and set long-range goals and make specific plans to achieve them.
_____ 2. I thoroughly enjoy counseling other people.
_____ 3. I love research and checking information, words and their definitions.
_____ 4. I have the ability to see needs other people don't notice.

_____ 5. I am sensitive to the emotional needs of others; I seem to know when they are hurting.

_____ 6. I am practical and short-term goals catch my interest.

_____ 7. I can spot a phony before other people discern one.

_____ 8. I am an organizer. I can take a series of tasks, organize them properly and help others to get organized, too.

_____ 9. I view problems as an opportunity for spiritual growth.

_____ 10. It is extremely important to me that words be used correctly.

_____ 11. I prefer to meet needs quietly without publicity.

_____ 12. I seem to be attracted to anyone who is in distress.

_____ 13. I am quickly aware of practical needs.

_____ 14. Everything is either black or white to me; there are no gray areas, especially where sin is concerned.

_____ 15. I can take a large job and easily break it down into minute details in order to reach a specific goal.

_____ 16. I am able to define positive steps for solving a problem or meeting a need.

_____ 17. It's easy for me to gather, organize, and retain a large amount of facts.

_____ 18. I can find great bargains, and any purchase I make is a wise one.

_____ 19. I have a deep desire to ease pain and to bring healing.

_____ 20. I enjoy being involved in hands-on projects.

_____ 21. I need outward evidence in a person's life to prove his inward heart change.

_____ 22. I can coordinate people and things (whatever it takes) to accomplish long-range goals.

_____ 23. I love to make practical applications for everyday life from Scripture.

_____ 24. I have a logical, objective approach to life.

_____ 25. Others follow my giving and give to my projects.

_____ 26. Prayer is a very important part of my life, even more so than many of my Christian friends.

_____ 27. I seem to have an extra measure of physical stamina.

_____ 28. I enjoy a lively debate and have the courage to stand firm on my beliefs even if I stand alone.

_____ 29. It's easy for me to delegate responsibility to other people.

_____ 30. I have the ability to verbally comfort the hurting.

_____ 31. I have to know the authority behind information. It bothers me when an illustration is used out of context.

_____ 32. I don't want to just give to a project; I want to be somewhat involved with the project, too.

_____ 33. I seem to know instinctively when people have sincere motives.

_____ 34. I am strongly motivated to complete any task I do. In fact, I readily look for shortcuts to get the job done quickly and efficiently.

_____ 35. I have an inner drive to communicate the truth of Scripture to everyone.

_____ 36. Pressure is my friend. In fact, pressure helps me get the job done, and I usually strive to finish it ahead of schedule.

_____ 37. I enjoy challenging the spiritually apathetic to grow in the Lord.

_____ 38. If someone comes to me with a problem, I would rather help her discover her own solution than give her a simple answer.

_____ 39. I don't like to be pressured into giving.

_____ 40. I can often see things from the other person's point of view; and when she talks to me, I actually *feel* her situation, often crying with her.

_____ 41. I would gladly inconvenience myself in order to help others, and I have a negative reaction to people who aren't willing to get involved.

_____ 42. Even with my direct, frank approach, I seem to be able to persuade people to my point of view, especially when God's Word is involved.

_____ 43. If there is a need, I can easily coordinate everything necessary to meet that need.

_____ 44. I enjoy being around other people.

_____ 45. I try to give detailed instructions to others so they will be able to follow exactly what I say.

_____ 46. What some people may see as selfishness is actually my personal thriftiness.

_____ 47. I receive a blessing from visiting hospitals, jails, nursing homes, or those who are shut-ins.

_____ 48. I'm involved in a number of activities and projects.

_____ 49. I don't like compromise and I have very strong opinions.

_____ 50. Most people can't keep up with me when I'm involved in a project. I push hard to reach my goals.

_____ 51. I am more interested in the essence rather than detail, so I may take some things out of context in order to press a point.

_____ 52. Learning new information is important to me, and I always want to know more.

_____ 53. I prefer any gift I give to have long-range value, not just meet an immediate need.

_____ 54. Working with the people who are ignored by others brings a special joy to me.

_____ 55. I believe that doing things cheerfully is one way to show my love.

_____ 56. People may think I am insensitive because I don't like to display my emotions in public.

_____ 57. I'm a project person. To me, getting the job done is more important than the individual people who are involved.

_____ 58. I want the people I counsel to overcome their problems so much that I sometimes get more involved in working out a solution than the counselee himself.

_____ 59. Finding the exact illustration that will add meaning to my instruction is important to me.

_____ 60. I don't like to be in debt to anyone for any reason.

_____ 61. I'd rather be around other people than be alone.

_____ 62. I am known as a good worker and willingly do whatever task needs doing.

_____ 63. I can show people where their blind spots are, and I want them to point out mine.

_____ 64. I'm not as sensitive to the needs of other people as I'd like to be. Often I don't see their hurts.

_____ 65. I can see what people can become with God's help, and I want to help them get there.

_____ 66. I find myself constantly correcting people around me. People sometimes say I'm too critical.

_____ 67. I don't mind living at a lower standard than my friends because it allows me to give more to God's work.

_____ 68. I have difficulty confronting people directly because I can't stand to hurt anyone either with words or actions. Consequently, others may view me as weak and indecisive.

_____ 69. I am a good follower and am very flexible.

_____ 70. I feel that a little showmanship doesn't hurt if it helps get my point across.

_____ 71. I tend to treat people the same way they treat me.

_____ 72. I hurt when others are hurting, and I want to help them turn to God for their answers.

_____ 73. Whenever I tell a story or pass along some information, I try to include all the details, no matter how small. I feel that details add depth of meaning.

_____ 74. Money management is easy for me, and I appear to do it well.

_____ 75. I can easily be hurt by the words and actions of others, which sometimes cause me to be depressed.

_____ 76. I have been known to let people take advantage of me.

_____ 77. Some people think I'm stubborn because I have a very strong will.

_____ 78. People sometimes see me as being bossy. I have to be careful not to be too pushy.

_____ 79. I enjoy changing people's attitudes from negative to positive whenever they are around me.

_____ 80. I don't take anything anyone says on face value. I need to know the *whys* as well as where the information came from.

_____ 81. For some reason I seem to be able to acquire money easily.

_____ 82. I seem to lack the ability to be firm and can't make decisions under stress.

_____ 83. Spiritual things tend to get lost in my focus on practical things.

_____ 84. It is very important to me to reveal sin and proclaim God's truth whether in a group or one to one.

_____ 85. I'm nit-picky about any job. Details are very important to me.

_____ 86. Even if someone has taken a nose-dive, I encourage her to get up and try again.

_____ 87. When I research something, I love to share that knowledge with others.

_____ 88. I don't give out of a sense of duty; giving money or things to God brings me deep pleasure, and I do it cheerfully.

_____ 89. I am more emotional than others around me, and I know my emotions affect the way I act.

_____ 90. Others may see me as a pushy person, but I just want to get the work done.

_____ 91. When I have a clear understanding of God's will, I don't hesitate to make it known to others.

Place each evaluation score in the appropriate box on the next page. Add the numbers in the boxes and place the total at the end of each line.

FINDING A MINISTRY YOU CAN LOVE

Add each column down and place total on the line below.

1.	2.	3.	4.	5.	6.	7.
8.	9.	10.	11.	12.	13.	14.
15.	16.	17.	18.	19.	20.	21.
22.	23.	24.	25.	26.	27.	28.
29.	30.	31.	32.	33.	34.	35.
36.	37.	38.	39.	40.	41.	42.
43.	44.	45.	46.	47.	48.	49.
50.	51.	52.	53.	54.	55.	56.
57.	58.	59.	60.	61.	62.	63.
64.	65.	66.	67.	68.	69.	70.
71.	72.	73.	74.	75.	76.	77.
78.	79.	80.	81.	82.	83.	84.
85.	86.	87.	88.	89.	90.	91.

1) ____ 2) ____ 3) ____ 4) ____ 5) ____ 6) ____ 7) ____

1) Administration   4) Giving   7) Prophesying
2) Encouraging   5) Mercy
3) Teaching   6) Serving

You probably had one or two scores that were higher than all the rest, while others fell into recognizable clusters. Remember, the higher score indicates how much of that gift you see in yourself. Circle the very top one (or two or three) and write them here:

1. _____

2. _____

3. _____

APPENDIX B

DISCOVERY EVALUATION

Read each statement through carefully and evaluate yourself on a scale of 0 to 5.

0 = doesn't describe me at all
1 = not very much
2 = occasionally
3 = sometimes
4 = usually
5 = describes me fully

_____ 1. I have the ability to perceive and set long-range goals and make specific plans to achieve them.
_____ 2. I thoroughly enjoy counseling other people.
_____ 3. I love research and checking information, words and their definitions.
_____ 4. I have the ability to see needs other people don't notice.

_____ 5. I am sensitive to the emotional needs of others; I seem to know when they are hurting.

_____ 6. I am practical and short-term goals catch my interest.

_____ 7. I can spot a phony before other people discern one.

_____ 8. I am an organizer. I can take a series of tasks, organize them properly and help others to get organized, too.

_____ 9. I view problems as an opportunity for spiritual growth.

_____ 10. It is extremely important to me that words be used correctly.

_____ 11. I prefer to meet needs quietly without publicity.

_____ 12. I seem to be attracted to anyone who is in distress.

_____ 13. I am quickly aware of practical needs.

_____ 14. Everything is either black or white to me; there are no gray areas, especially where sin is concerned.

_____ 15. I can take a large job and easily break it down into minute details in order to reach a specific goal.

_____ 16. I am able to define positive steps for solving a problem or meeting a need.

_____ 17. It's easy for me to gather, organize, and retain a large amount of facts.

_____ 18. I can find great bargains, and any purchase I make is a wise one.

_____ 19. I have a deep desire to ease pain and to bring healing.

_____ 20. I enjoy being involved in hands-on projects.

_____ 21. I need outward evidence in a person's life to prove his inward heart change.

_____ 22. I can coordinate people and things (whatever it takes) to accomplish long-range goals.

_____ 23. I love to make practical applications for everyday life from Scripture.

_____ 24. I have a logical, objective approach to life.

_____ 25. Others follow my giving and give to my projects.

_____ 26. Prayer is a very important part of my life, even more so than many of my Christian friends.

_____ 27. I seem to have an extra measure of physical stamina.

_____ 28. I enjoy a lively debate and have the courage to stand firm on my beliefs even if I stand alone.

_____ 29. It's easy for me to delegate responsibility to other people.

_____ 30. I have the ability to verbally comfort the hurting.

_____ 31. I have to know the authority behind information. It bothers me when an illustration is used out of context.

_____ 32. I don't want to just give to a project; I want to be somewhat involved with the project, too.

_____ 33. I seem to know instinctively when people have sincere motives.

_____ 34. I am strongly motivated to complete any task I do. In fact, I readily look for shortcuts to get the job done quickly and efficiently.

_____ 35. I have an inner drive to communicate the truth of Scripture to everyone.

_____ 36. Pressure is my friend. In fact, pressure helps me get the job done, and I usually strive to finish it ahead of schedule.

_____ 37. I enjoy challenging the spiritually apathetic to grow in the Lord.

_____ 38. If someone comes to me with a problem, I would rather help her discover her own solution than give her a simple answer.

_____ 39. I don't like to be pressured into giving.

_____ 40. I can often see things from the other person's point of view; and when she talks to me, I actually *feel* her situation, often crying with her.

_____ 41. I would gladly inconvenience myself in order to help others, and I have a negative reaction to people who aren't willing to get involved.

_____ 42. Even with my direct, frank approach, I seem to be able to persuade people to my point of view, especially when God's Word is involved.

_____ 43. If there is a need, I can easily coordinate everything necessary to meet that need.

_____ 44. I enjoy being around other people.

_____ 45. I try to give detailed instructions to others so they will be able to follow exactly what I say.

_____ 46. What some people may see as selfishness is actually my personal thriftiness.

_____ 47. I receive a blessing from visiting hospitals, jails, nursing homes, or those who are shut-ins.

_____ 48. I'm involved in a number of activities and projects.

_____ 49. I don't like compromise and I have very strong opinions.

_____ 50. Most people can't keep up with me when I'm involved in a project. I push hard to reach my goals.

_____ 51. I am more interested in the essence rather than detail, so I may take some things out of context in order to press a point.

_____ 52. Learning new information is important to me, and I always want to know more.

_____ 53. I prefer any gift I give to have long-range value, not just meet an immediate need.

_____ 54. Working with the people who are ignored by others brings a special joy to me.

_____ 55. I believe that doing things cheerfully is one way to show my love.

_____ 56. People may think I am insensitive because I don't like to display my emotions in public.

_____ 57. I'm a project person. To me, getting the job done is more important than the individual people who are involved.

_____ 58. I want the people I counsel to overcome their problems so much that I sometimes get more involved in working out a solution than the counselee himself.

_____ 59. Finding the exact illustration that will add meaning to my instruction is important to me.

_____ 60. I don't like to be in debt to anyone for any reason.

_____ 61. I'd rather be around other people than be alone.

_____ 62. I am known as a good worker and willingly do whatever task needs doing.

_____ 63. I can show people where their blind spots are, and I want them to point out mine.

_____ 64. I'm not as sensitive to the needs of other people as I'd like to be. Often I don't see their hurts.

_____ 65. I can see what people can become with God's help, and I want to help them get there.

_____ 66. I find myself constantly correcting people around me. People sometimes say I'm too critical.

_____ 67. I don't mind living at a lower standard than my friends because it allows me to give more to God's work.

_____ 68. I have difficulty confronting people directly because I can't stand to hurt anyone either with words or actions. Consequently, others may view me as weak and indecisive.

_____ 69. I am a good follower and am very flexible.

_____ 70. I feel that a little showmanship doesn't hurt if it helps get my point across.

_____ 71. I tend to treat people the same way they treat me.

_____ 72. I hurt when others are hurting, and I want to help them turn to God for their answers.

_____ 73. Whenever I tell a story or pass along some information, I try to include all the details, no matter how small. I feel that details add depth of meaning.

_____ 74. Money management is easy for me, and I appear to do it well.

_____ 75. I can easily be hurt by the words and actions of others, which sometimes cause me to be depressed.

_____ 76. I have been known to let people take advantage of me.

_____ 77. Some people think I'm stubborn because I have a very strong will.

_____ 78. People sometimes see me as being bossy. I have to be careful not to be too pushy.

_____ 79. I enjoy changing people's attitudes from negative to positive whenever they are around me.

_____ 80. I don't take anything anyone says on face value. I need to know the *whys* as well as where the information came from.

_____ 81. For some reason I seem to be able to acquire money easily.

_____ 82. I seem to lack the ability to be firm and can't make decisions under stress.

_____ 83. Spiritual things tend to get lost in my focus on practical things.

_____ 84. It is very important to me to reveal sin and proclaim God's truth whether in a group or one to one.

_____ 85. I'm nit-picky about any job. Details are very important to me.

_____ 86. Even if someone has taken a nose-dive, I encourage her to get up and try again.

_____ 87. When I research something, I love to share that knowledge with others.

_____ 88. I don't give out of a sense of duty; giving money or things to God brings me deep pleasure, and I do it cheerfully.

_____ 89. I am more emotional than others around me, and I know my emotions affect the way I act.

_____ 90. Others may see me as a pushy person, but I just want to get the work done.

_____ 91. When I have a clear understanding of God's will, I don't hesitate to make it known to others.

Place each evaluation score in the appropriate box on the next page. Add the numbers in the boxes and place the total at the end of each line.

FINDING A MINISTRY YOU CAN LOVE

Add each column down and place total on the line below.

1.	2.	3.	4.	5.	6.	7.
8.	9.	10.	11.	12.	13.	14.
15.	16.	17.	18.	19.	20.	21.
22.	23.	24.	25.	26.	27.	28.
29.	30.	31.	32.	33.	34.	35.
36.	37.	38.	39.	40.	41.	42.
43.	44.	45.	46.	47.	48.	49.
50.	51.	52.	53.	54.	55.	56.
57.	58.	59.	60.	61.	62.	63.
64.	65.	66.	67.	68.	69.	70.
71.	72.	73.	74.	75.	76.	77.
78.	79.	80.	81.	82.	83.	84.
85.	86.	87.	88.	89.	90.	91.

1)   2)   3)   4)   5)   6)   7)

1) Administration   4) Giving   7) Prophesying
2) Encouraging   5) Mercy
3) Teaching   6) Serving

You probably had one or two scores that were higher than all the rest, while others fell into recognizable clusters. Remember, the higher score indicates how much of that gift you see in yourself. Circle the very top one (or two or three) and write them here:

1. _____

2. _____

3. _____